$martEssentials™

for BUYING A HOME

More Titles In Best-Selling SMART ESSENTIALS™ Series

$martEssentials™

for BUYING A HOME

How To Get The Best Price And The Lowest Payment

Amy J. Hausman

Dan Gooder Richard
SMART ESSENTIALS Series Editor

Inkspiration Media

SMART ESSENTIALS™ FOR BUYING A HOME:
How To Get The Best Price And The Lowest Payment

Published by:
Inkspiration Media
2724 Dorr Avenue, Suite 103, Fairfax, VA 22031
http://www.SmartEssentials.com

ISTC: A0320120000B474A
Library of Congress Control Number: 2012955330

Publisher's Cataloging-In-Publication Data
(Prepared by The Donohue Group, Inc.)

Hausman, Amy J., 1971 –
   Smart Essentials™ for buying a home : how to get the best price
and the lowest payment / Amy J. Hausman.
      p. ; cm. — (Smart Essentials™ series)
   ISBN-13: 978-1-939319-02-9
   ISBN-10: 1-939319-02-1
   1. House buying — United States. 2. Residential real estate —
Purchasing — United States. I. Title. II. Title: Buying a home
HD259 .H38 2013
643/.12/0973   2012955330

CONTENTS

UPFRONT

What You'll Take Away

We know you're smart. (Reading SMART ESSENTIALS FOR BUYING A HOME proves it . . . at least to us.) And we know your time is precious.

In this no-fluff SMART ESSENTIALS guide, you'll take away concise, practical, insider strategies to do three things:

- ▶ Buy the home of your dreams for the best price.
- ▶ Save money and time buying a home that fits your needs for the lowest monthly payment.
- ▶ Avoid the costly mistakes even smart home buyers make.

We Respect Your Time

We call this a SMART ESSENTIALS guide because it includes everything you need to know once you decide to purchase a home— and doesn't waste your time on extraneous filler. We spare you the side trips, such as noodling the decision to buy or not, how to repair your credit, sample contracts and check-the-box inspector reports, settlement documents explained line by line, weighing buying over renting, sticky-dot moving tips, blah, blah, blah. Why? Because you don't need to become a real estate expert. You just need the essential, up-to-date and relevant information to make smart decisions throughout the home buying process *and* to ask the right questions of the professionals on your home buying team—your agent/broker, loan officer, inspectors, settlement agent, etc. We keep your eyes on the prize: Buying the perfect home at the best price and lowest payment.

How This SMART ESSENTIALS Is Organized

After learning the essentials of how to BUY SMART, there are six key decisions you must get right from the start, which shapes the following sections of your SMART ESSENTIALS guide:

🔊 **TEAM:** Find the right buyer's agent and mortgage professional to be the core of your home buying team.

🔊 **BUDGET:** Figure out the biggest loan you can get, but actually buy the best home for you that you can afford.

- **MONEY:** Nail down the perfect loan that is right for your financial situation.

- **SHOP:** Preview only homes that fit your budget and lifestyle. (Time is money.)

- **NEGOTIATE:** Craft your offer and play your counteroffers to get the best contract.

- **CLOSE:** Avoid costly mistakes that can torpedo your purchase in the home stretch.

Most Important: We Want To Hear From You. Often.

Nothing informs our readers as much as stories from other Smarties . . . what they did right, stupid mistakes they can laugh about (now) and advice on tricky choices they had to make along the road of good intentions. Come back regularly to our website at *http://www.SmartEssentials.com*. Share your story. Check out the amazing tips and slips other Smarties experienced. We love your stories! And, we know other Smarties do too.

CHAPTER 1
BUY SMART

Buying a home is far from simple or easy, especially in today's toughest markets. It can be difficult to stay focused on the essentials . . . and not being distracted by the collateral chatter that surrounds one of life's most important purchases.

To buy a home today, you need to avoid the costly, sometimes painful mistakes other home buyers have made before you. You can avoid problems by paying attention to the following essential lessons other buyers have had to learn the hard way.

12 ESSENTIAL KEYS TO BUYING A HOME

1. **Check your credit before you apply for a loan.** Before you apply for a mortgage and start touring homes, make sure your credit is in good shape. You can get a free look at your credit reports from the big three credit reporting agencies — Equifax, Experian and TransUnion — by going online to *www.AnnualCreditReport.com*. (Although the reports are free once per year, you'll have to pay a small fee to see your actual credit score.) Several months before you plan to apply for a mortgage, do what you can to improve your credit score if it isn't in the excellent range — 740 or higher. You may need to pay off credit cards, redistribute your debt and/or correct errors in your credit reports.

2. **Plan your housing budget realistically.** (1) Figure out how much cash you have on hand to put toward a down payment and closing costs. (2) List all the expenses you'll incur as a homeowner (except your monthly payment for principal and interest), including estimated property taxes, insurance, utilities, maintenance, repairs and new furnishings. (Don't worry: We'll show you how to find accurate figures for your situation in Chapter 3.) (3) Add your other regular expenses for car payments and loans, transportation, clothing, food, recreation, medical care, college fees, retirement savings, etc. (4) Subtract the above expenses from income. (5) What's left over will be the realistic monthly housing payment

you can comfortably afford — even if you're tempted to borrow more and are approved to do so.

3. **Gather information.** Find out about the home buying process so you're comfortable each step of the way. How? Keep reading. Then, investigate and review local property data to get an idea of price points, listing-to-sales-price ratios, hottest areas and best places for a bargain. Research schools in the area you are interested in. A wealth of information is available online, at your local library, in books and eBooks about home buying or by contacting a buyer's agent real estate professional. Although a real estate agent can help guide you through the process, learning the lingo and standard local practices beforehand will help keep the cork on your stress level. Your buyer specialist will provide up-to-the-minute stats of what comparable properties sell for in specific neighborhoods and what impact various features have on price.

4. **Get pre-approval for a mortgage before you begin home shopping.** In today's marketplace, touring homes without knowing your buying power is a waste of everyone's time . . . especially yours. Getting loan pre-approval eliminates surprises and saves you valuable time. Additionally, home sellers can smell an unqualified buyer from the curb and prefer to work with buyers who already have a mortgage commitment from a lender. Starting out knowing exactly what you can borrow for a home (instead of the wishful thinking a "pre-qualification" provides) will help you narrow your search to the price range you can afford. Finally, being pre-approved for a loan shortens the time to closing or settlement once you strike a deal with the home seller.

5. **Select the right loan.** If you only plan to live in the home five years or less, you may want an adjustable-rate mortgage, which often carries the lowest interest rate available. Cash-strapped buyers will want to look for a low-down-payment program, but should factor in the cost of private mortgage insurance (PMI). Compare interest rates using APR (Annual Percentage Rate). (More about PMI and APR in Chapter 4 MONEY.) Be sure to calculate how much each option will cost you monthly and during the entire period you're likely to own the home. Simply put: You'll need a professional mortgage lender to help you compare different loan products to find which one best fits your financial situation. We'll show you how to find that lender.

6. **List what you must have in a home first, then prioritize your wants. Think ahead.** Consider changes that might affect your housing requirements in the next several years. Remember, though, if you're buying your first home, it doesn't have to meet your needs or dreams for a lifetime; after building some equity, you should someday be in a position to sell your home and buy another. (More in Chapter 5 SHOP.)

7. **Select a top-notch buyer's real estate professional.** Ask friends, neighbors, family members and co-workers for recommendations. Read reviews online. Visit the online presence of the real estate pros you're considering and check for Facebook and LinkedIn pages. Observe their responsiveness and interactions. Although it's valuable to talk with several agents first, you'll be best served working with one top agent you have a good rapport with, one who knows the local market and listens closely to your needs. Hiring a buyer's agent who will be legally bound to represent your interests in the transaction — not the seller's — is essential.

8. **Don't buy on impulse.** First-time buyers sometimes rush into the first home they find that, at first glance, appears to meet their needs and budget. It's a costly mistake to choose the wrong home — one that's too big or too small for future needs; that's a fixer-upper if you're not handy; that's too far from work or too close to traffic; that's likely to need extensive rehab; or that's in the wrong price range.

Spend time looking around until you have at least three or four good candidates, then take a closer, deeper look. Drill into what utilities will cost. Consider resale value of the location carefully. (Location is the one thing you can't fix.) Ask yourself whether your furniture will fit in the home. Research zoning restrictions, homeowners association rules and plans for development/redevelopment in the area. Hiring a professional home inspector is always a good idea to put a fine point on how much fixing-up you're comfortable with and avoid purchasing a money pit with hidden problems that can cost you major bucks down the road.

9. **Be flexible during negotiations.** Sellers may have some requirements — e.g., a particular closing date, taking the dining room chandelier, etc. — that won't cost you much to comply with. Remember, buying a home is not a contest between you and the seller; it's an agreement that must meet both parties' needs.

---

10. **Avoid making major purchases or applying for more credit.**
Your lender will underwrite your loan based on a snapshot of your
finances just before settlement or closing. That picture will change
for the worse if it appears you're looking for additional credit or you
deplete your cash stash. (We'll help you avoid some never-do's that
can sabotage your closing at the last minute.)

11. **Stay in close contact with your loan officer and real estate
agent.** Once you sign a contract to purchase, you'll supply a blizzard
of paperwork, purchase homeowners insurance, make appointments
for inspections and deal with a dozen other details. Not to mention
packing to move! Be sure to ask questions if you don't understand
what's going on or what you need to do next. That's why you hired
the pros!

12. **Buy owner's title insurance.** Most lenders require you to
purchase a lender's title policy to cover their interests in the event
that someone else comes forward with a claim to the property after
closing or settlement. To protect your interests, you'll need to buy a
separate owner's title policy.

TOP TIPS TO HOME SHOP SMARTER, FASTER, CHEAPER

Most home buyers today are looking for a great price, energy efficiency,
functionality and comfort in the home they purchase. Yet finding all the
right features in the perfect location can be harder than expected . . .
despite a wide selection.

When you're in the market to buy a home, shopping for a home in
your price range is a straightforward procedure. Finding the right-size
home in the right condition and the right area is worth the search. One
reason home shopping can be a challenge is the "downsizing" trend in
recent years in new-home construction. To keep costs down and meet
marketplace demands, builders have been trading size for lower sales
prices, nicer amenities and better locations. On the other hand, that may
work perfectly for *you*.

Need storage? Want cozy? Prefer energy efficiency? No matter what's
top on your list, here are eight tips to help you make the best decisions.
Use these proven pointers and you can move into your next home faster,
cheaper and more simply than you might imagine.

1. **Do your homework.** Take time to do online research about neighborhoods that interest you. Then test drive and walk them in person. For amenities that are important to you and your family — work, schools, shopping, parks, playgrounds, etc. — figure out how far they are from the area you're considering. Drive routes during rush hour to get a realistic sense of commute times.

2. **Be prepared.** Before you start viewing homes, secure your down payment. This is worth repeating: Know exactly how much you can afford by getting pre-approved for a home mortgage. This tip alone will make your purchase offer more inviting to sellers, as they will know you have your financing elements already in place.

3. **Stay flexible.** Don't box in your needs for a home. If you're looking for a home office, consider extra bedrooms, dens, unfinished spaces in basements or attics, or even dividing a large room to carve out office space. Ditto for play areas for young children or space to host guests. Even if a listing doesn't specify the perfect configuration, if everything else seems like a good fit, take a look at what the home holds that could fulfill your needs completely.

4. **Go green to save.** Not everyone is an eco-warrior, but who doesn't want to save a little cash? Look for energy-efficient systems and features in the homes you view — or determine if they can be retrofitted with energy-saving elements later on. ENERGY STAR appliances and other energy-saving labels will alert you to money-saving features. Ask the home sellers for previous utility bills to see the true costs of operating the home.

5. **Prioritize rooms.** Consider and rank the importance of rooms and features in the home you are looking for. Is the four-bedrooms requirement a must or a would-like? Is an eat-in kitchen necessary, or would a counter area that seats four be sufficient? Is a first-floor master bedroom totally a deal breaker? Understand the "wants versus needs" on your house hunting list before you set out. That way, when you find that gem of a home, you'll be ready to make an immediate offer.

6. **Look ahead.** If the homes you view are hard to see past the clutter, needed repairs or personal belongings, take a moment to step back and imagine what your furniture and belongings will look like in the space. Don't be overwhelmed when not seeing a perfectly staged

home. By looking beyond the existing contents of a home, you may find the perfect home — and get it for a great price — because no one else can see through the owners' stuff.

7. **Don't forget the formalities.** No matter what your concerns, consider your home-inspection money well spent. Be sure to attend the inspection, if possible, because you'll learn a lot about the property. Then read the entire report. Be sure your purchase contract accommodates your decision for a home inspection so your new home doesn't come with costly repair surprises. To find bargains, home buyers should look beyond price . . . including location, terms, condition and amenities offered.

HOME BUYING 101 ESSENTIAL TRUTHS

Home buyers and sellers often bring misinformation to the table when it's time to strike a real estate deal. While well-meaning friends and neighbors may have your best interests at heart when they pass along a tip, you'd be wise to get the facts straight from your real estate agent. Here are a few of the myths that crop up for home buyers — and often get in the way.

Myth: *Being pre-qualified for a loan is the same as being pre-approved.*

Reality: When lenders pre-qualify home buyers, they simply run a few numbers to determine an approximate purchase price a buyer can afford — no lending commitment is in effect. Home sellers prefer a buyer who is *pre-approved* because it means the lender has already collected and analyzed most of the documents and information necessary to make a loan commitment, assuming a few additional requirements are met (type of property, maintained credit rating, etc.).

Myth: *Overpriced homes leave sellers room for inevitable negotiations.*

Reality: If a home is priced right, you won't have to negotiate! You will have looked at other homes in the area, you will know what the home you're considering is worth and you'll be able to craft your offer accordingly. Though sellers may still try to negotiate, offer only a realistic price that fits your budget and meets with comparable homes in the vicinity.

BUY SMART

Myth: *It's better to wait to buy the perfect, dream home than settle for a lesser home that fits in the current budget.*

Reality: If you have the cash and credit to purchase a home, be realistic about what it will buy in your area of interest. Remember: There's no time like the present. Most buyers benefit from home appreciation, which leverages a relatively small down-payment investment into a nice return at sale time — when you may be able to move up to a home that is closer to your idea of perfection. If you fool yourself into waiting for what is truly unattainable given your resources, you'll miss some attractive opportunities that may also become out of reach as weeks and months pass by.

Myth: *Qualified buyers should be able to get their own financing and not rely on seller financing.*

Reality: Sellers sometimes offer financing that can help young buyers and those with limited cash or less-than-perfect credit, who can't afford to purchase a home with lender financing. Offering financing can help sellers get their homes sold in tough markets without dropping the price below market value. Other sellers may offer rent-to-buy or lease-purchase deals.

Myth: *A home will appraise at the same value whether it is in good condition or not.*

Reality: Although square footage, number of rooms and other non-cosmetic features determine a home's baseline value compared with properties recently sold in the area, appraisers will factor the home's condition into the final appraised value. More important, a home's condition will determine how many buyers become interested in the home and how motivated they are to buy it. Most buyers — like you — prefer homes in move-in condition. Those that need more work frequently sell below market prices.

Now let's cut to the chase. First stop: Find and hire a top-notch, professional team using the information in Chapter 2.

Chapter 1 Roundup

Smart Essentials BUY SMART :: What You Have Learned

▶▶ Check and fix your credit before you apply for a mortgage.

▶▶ Focus on the 12 essential keys to buying a home.

▶▶ Being pre-approved for a mortgage beats simply being pre-qualified.

▶▶ With the right approach, you can buy a home smarter, faster and cheaper.

▶▶ Planning and information gathering help smooth the home buying process.

▶▶ Home buying myths can prevent you from buying the home you want.

CHAPTER 2

TEAM

In this chapter, you'll learn smart ways to:

1. Know what a real estate agent can do for you.

2. Hire a buyer's agent to represent your interests with no cost to you.

3. Select a lender that offers a loan program that fits your financial situation.

TEAM PART 1: SELECT A TOP-NOTCH REALTOR®

No matter where you're looking to buy a home, it's essential to work with a top-notch real estate professional to secure your new home. Choosing the right "buyer's agent" to help you purchase a home is almost as important as picking the right house! It used to be that all real estate agents worked for home sellers. In today's market, the buyer can hire an agent, too.

All agents are bound by law to deal fairly and ethically with both buyer and seller. Some buyers may choose to sign a contract to work with a buyer's agent, whose legal obligation is to represent the interests of the buyer. A buyer's agent, whose fee or commission is typically paid by the seller (although buyer-paid arrangements aren't unheard of), is able to negotiate sale price and terms on behalf of the buyer.

A buyer's agent can service you in many ways, such as:

🦴 Helping you set up a plan of action through an analysis of your needs and your finances, the current housing market, homes available in your price range and lenders' mortgage options.

🦴 Personally conducting your search to find neighborhoods and homes that fit your requirements.

🦴 Guiding you through the intricacies of making an offer on a home and presenting your offer to the seller.

🦴 Assisting you through both the pre-settlement/pre-closing and settlement/closing processes.

CHAPTER 2

TEAM

◆ ◆ ◆

Essential Takeaway

Essential Takeaway: A buyer's agent is someone in your corner, looking after your best interests (rather than the seller's). Your best bet for finding your new home is working with a real estate agent who really knows the area where you're looking to buy. A neighborhood specialist can give you the most-current data about the area to ensure you're looking at homes that fit your budget. If you have more questions than the agent can answer, a top agent will know where to get the answers you need.

◆ ◆ ◆

What You Need To Know About Your Real Estate Agent

While you may be tempted to work with the first agent you interview, consider that buying a home is one of the most important financial decisions you'll ever make. Be sure to interview several agents before signing a buyer-broker agreement.

Smart questions to ask agents before you hire one:

1. Can you provide me with a copy of your buyer's agency agreement to review? (Be sure to ask follow-up questions after reading the document.)

2. How long have you worked in the area where I'm looking for a home?

3. How long have you been a real estate agent? How long have you been with your current brokerage?

4. Do you work exclusively as a buyer's agent, or do you also work with sellers? How do you handle transactions where the buyer you represent wants to purchase a home that you or your brokerage has listed for the seller?

5. How many buyer's agreements did you work with during the past year?

6. How many transactions did you close last year for home buyers you worked with? (Also called "buyer-side transactions.")

7. How much do your services cost? (If not paid by the seller, a flat fee may be required or the fee may be specified as a percentage of the home's sale price. Find out under what scenarios you would have to pay the commission.)

8. What is your preferred method of communication? (Telephone, e-mail, Facebook messages, texts, Twitter messages, in-person. Determine if their answer corresponds to your preferred method. You don't want to work with someone who won't—or can't— accept your late-night texts!)

9. When are you available to show homes? (If, for some reason, the agent's availability is narrow—and you work long or odd hours— ensure that you will be able to meet up with the agent to tour homes at mutually agreeable times.)

10. What's your general plan of action? How will you determine what homes are best suited—and affordable—for my needs? How will you provide me with new listings as they come on the market?

When interviewing agents, ask for references from the three most recent transactions. Contact these clients to ask how they felt about their experience. Ask both broad and specific questions:

▶ How well does the agent communicate?

▶ Do you think you received sound advice?

▶ Did the agent return your calls/e-mails promptly?

▶ Did anything go wrong during the transaction?

▶ Is there anything you wish the agent had handled differently?

▶ Would you work with this agent again—why or why not?

Be aware: When you sign a buyer's agent agreement, the contract is with the broker/company rather than the specific sales associate. *Smart Tip:* Before you sign, be sure to negotiate an understanding on how to end the contract—a cancellation clause—should the agent and/or broker fail to meet your expectations. Most brokers are willing to release buyers from the contract with notice of 24 to 48 hours; however, the broker will retain right to compensation—through a protection clause—should you subsequently buy a property, within a specified time frame, that was introduced to you by the agent or brokerage.

◆ ◆ ◆

Essential Takeaway

Essential Takeaway: If you have a home to sell, and it's in the same city where you're looking to buy, this same real estate professional may be able to handle your sale transaction as well! Knowing the big picture, this single agent is in the best position to coordinate the timing of your sale and purchase, and help you negotiate contract terms that coordinate the two transactions. If you're a twofer: Ask for a discount on the listing commission side—that's the expensive one you pay for.

◆ ◆ ◆

TEAM PART 2: SELECT AN OUTSTANDING LENDER

When you're in the market to buy a home, unless you are paying cash, it's essential to compare lenders to find the best rate and terms for your mortgage. Think about it: Just as you will look at different homes on the market, it's important to check all the financing options available. Depending on your particular situation, the traditional 30-year, fixed-interest-rate loan may not be the best option for your home purchase.

According to a recent survey by Harris Interactive and LendingTree, 40% of home buyers obtain only one mortgage-loan quote before making their decision on a lender. That's dumb. Understandably, not having done much comparison shopping, only about a quarter (28%) of those surveyed feel they got the best rate and terms.

Mortgage shopping can be frustrating and complex—especially if you have never done it before or haven't done it recently. But when you're considering a financial commitment for many years to come, you owe it to yourself to find the loan package that best fits your needs. All loans are not created equal, and borrowing costs aren't the same either.

Types of Mortgage Companies

A number of different types of companies offer home mortgage loans. Not every mortgage provider offers every type of loan option. With that in mind, here is a brief summary of how they operate:

● **Mortgage bankers** are direct lenders, who use their own funds to originate loans, then often quickly sell the loans on the secondary mortgage market. They may or may not continue to service the loans (sending bills, statements, etc.) after selling them. Typically, the loans they provide meet guidelines established by Fannie Mae and Freddie Mac†† or other government programs that secure loans, so the loans can be easily sold in the secondary mortgage market. (Most home buyers work with mortgage bankers.)

> ††*Fannie Mae And Freddie Mac*
> First the names . . . Fannie Mae was a nickname (now its official name) given to the Federal National Mortgage Association, authorized by Congress in 1938 as part of the New Deal. The Federal Home Loan Mortgage Corporation— nicknamed Freddie Mac—came along in 1970. Both government-sponsored enterprises (GSEs) were designed to expand the secondary market for mortgages so that originating lenders (those actually providing funds for loans) could sell their loans and thus replenish their funds to make more loans. The GSEs accomplish this by either purchasing mortgages or guaranteeing mortgages owned by other investors—provided the mortgages conform to Fannie/Freddie standards. The mission of Fannie Mae and Freddie Mac is to make homeownership more affordable for the average Joe and Jane.

● **Portfolio lenders** are also direct lenders, using their own funds to make loans. Rather than selling their loans, they typically keep them as investments—at least for a period of time. Because resale isn't the goal, portfolio lenders are not as bound by Fannie Mae/Freddie Mac guidelines. That leeway can make these lenders more flexible. Some institutions, such as banks, savings and loans or credit unions, may operate both as mortgage bankers and portfolio lenders.

● **Mortgage brokers** work with a number of lenders, and therefore can offer a wide variety of loan programs. Serving as an intermediary between lenders and borrowers, the mortgage broker will help the borrower select a loan program, then will look for a lender to fund the loan. The broker works with the borrower to complete a loan application, collect required documentation, order a credit report, arrange to have the property appraised, etc. Payment for the broker is factored into the cost of the loan, usually as "origination" or "underwriting" fees in closing/settlement costs[tt].

> [tt] ***Closing/Settlement***
> At closing or settlement (also, "closing escrow" depending on your area) all parties review and sign the documents used in the real estate transaction for a successful transfer of ownership. A "closing sheet" summary document is prepared by a closing agent or attorney detailing the fees, commissions, insurance, and other transaction amounts. Save this document, known as the HUD-1 Settlement Statement, in your files.

● **Correspondent mortgage brokers** act as agents for a single lender (but sometimes several) from loan origination through settlement/closing. The loans are made in the correspondent's name even though the lender supplies the funds, usually underwrites the loan and owns the loan after closing/settlement. The correspondent may also become the servicer for the lender. Correspondents often are paid from the loan origination fee charged to the borrower.

How To Size Up A Top-Quality Mortgage Professional

No matter what type of lender you work with, be sure to bust the chops of every mortgage professional in an interview before you commit to working with them. The scary part is that until recently, less licensing/training was required of loan officers than of real estate agents. It's smart to talk to several mortgage professionals and find out which is the best fit for you based on your financial needs. There's no way around it — ask the hard questions:

1. How long have you been a mortgage professional? How long have you been with the current company? Are you registered as a mortgage originator?

2. What kind of company is your mortgage firm? (See earlier descriptions of banker, lender, broker.)

3. How long is the lock period on your loans? Do you provide lock-ins in writing? Do you charge a lock-in fee — and if so, how much?

4. When can you provide me with a Good Faith Estimate[tt] of loan costs?

⁺⁺ *Good Faith Estimate (GFE)*

You have the right to ask lenders for a Good Faith Estimate of all loan and settlement/closing charges *before* you agree to a loan or pay any fees (other than for a credit report). According to the Real Estate Settlement Procedures Act (RESPA), lenders have three days after you apply for a loan to provide you with a standardized GFE, but may not charge you for anything more than the cost of a credit report (about $15 to $30) until after the GFE is issued and you agree to the loan.

5. What is your preferred method of communication — telephone, e-mail, fax, in-person? (Applying for a loan means supplying the lender with an avalanche of documents. Determine if answers to this question fit with your situation and preferred method. Find out how often the loan officer will keep you updated. Will he/she give you a direct phone number or cell-phone number you can call?)

6. What loan products and interest rates do you offer? (Important question you should ask early in the process.)

7. How quickly can mortgage pre-approval be processed?

8. How long is it currently taking you to close a loan?

9. (To mortgage brokers . . .) How much will you be paid by me and the lender for my loan?

10. Are you equipped to approve loans in-house? Or are applications sent to a home office?

Be sure to get references from recent loan clients you can contact. Ask them how they felt about the experience. Just like real estate agent testimonials, both broad and specific questions give previous customers openings to talk and to focus their replies:

▶ How well does the loan officer communicate?

▶ Do you think you received sound advice?

▶ Did the loan officer return your calls promptly?

▶ Did anything go wrong during the transaction?

▶ Is there anything you wish the loan officer had handled differently?

▶ Would you work with this loan officer again? Why or why not?
▶ Would you work with this mortgage company again? Why or why not?

◆ ◆ ◆

Essential Takeaway

Essential Takeaway: You'll learn plenty about loan costs in Chapter 4 MONEY. Be aware that there's a range of garden-variety closing/settlement costs: loan fees, pre-paids, escrows, title fees, recording fees and settlement fees. Loan fees, specifically, include fees for origination, lender's inspection and mortgage broker fees, as well as appraisal, credit report, mortgage insurance or assumption fees. What you want to drill into during interviews is the origination, lender's inspection, broker fees (if any) and any other fees (what some call "junk fees"). Simply: Know how the lender makes money, and you will have a yardstick with which to make your lender selection.

◆ ◆ ◆

Loan-Program Choice Will Dictate Lender Choice

There's no way around it: Different buyers have different mortgage needs. Be smart and research the various types of loan programs available to decide on the loan type you want *before* you finally pick a lender to work with. (We'll talk more extensively about types of loan programs in Chapter 4.) If you need help deciding on a loan type, good mortgage professionals will run the numbers with you for all your mortgage options — or at least the ones they offer — at no charge to you.

Once you've definitely decided on a loan type, start interviewing only lenders who offer that loan type so you can compare their interest rates, costs, terms and services. Don't allow yourself to be sidetracked into quotes on a loan option you've already considered and rejected. You want to compare apples to apples — not apples to oranges to pears.

TEAM

You'll run into a troop of other pros in your home buying adventure. But by far, the two most essential members of your team are a top buyer's agent and an outstanding loan officer. Get those right, and you'll be well on your way to buying smart.

Next, it's time to get organized. The most helpful tool in your kit is developing a budget. There, we said it . . . the "B" word. It's not as bad as you think. We'll show you how in Chapter 3.

Chapter 2 Roundup

Smart Essentials TEAM :: What You Have Learned

▶▶ What you need to know to select a top-notch buyer's agent.

▶▶ Questions to ask before you hire your real estate agent.

▶▶ Why a top lender is essential to your home buying team.

▶▶ Different types of mortgage loans come from different types of providers.

▶▶ How to size up an outstanding mortgage professional.

▶▶ Why your loan program choice will dictate your lender choice.

Smart Essentials

Page   **Essential Note**

CHAPTER 3

BUDGET

In this chapter, you'll learn smart ways to:

1. Boost your credit to earn a gold-star credit score and increase your buying power.

2. Get your down payment and closing cash together in one place.

3. Nail down a budget that is affordable and avoids costly mistakes.

NURTURE YOUR CREDIT LIKE YOUR FIRST BORN

When you're looking to purchase a home, it's just dumb not to check your credit first. Do it now — before you apply for a loan and before you start looking at homes. You can get a free credit report once a year from each of the big-three credit reporting agencies — Equifax, Experian or TransUnion — at *http://www.AnnualCreditReport.com.*

FICO[††] credit scores range from 300 to 850. Do what you can to improve your credit score if it isn't in the excellent range — which most lenders agree is about 740 and above. Ask your lender if they use FICO credit scores to evaluate your creditworthiness, or whether they use one of the other services, such as VantageScore (501 to 990) or CE Score (350 to 850).

> [††] *FICO*
> FICO is the most commonly used credit scoring model, developed by Fair Isaac and Company, to calculate credit scores based on credit-report information compiled by the big-three credit agencies — though there are other scoring models as well.

◆ ◆ ◆

Essential Takeaway

Essential Takeaway: Each credit reporting company must supply you with a free credit report once annually. That means you can effectively check your credit history three times per year for free by selecting just one company's report every four months. That said, not all credit reporting companies have exactly the same information about you. Be smart. If you're considering applying for credit or a loan, ask the provider which report they'll review to determine your qualifications to borrow. Then check that company's credit report online and be sure to correct any errors or explain any problematic late/overdue amounts you see on your credit report.

◆ ◆ ◆

30-Second Course To Power Up Your Credit

Before you sign your life away to a mortgage, take the next 30-second course. You'll learn seven easy steps to power-up your credit before you apply for a mortgage. After all, the better your credit looks and the higher your score, the more you'll qualify to borrow and the lower your interest rate will be. Here's a quick peek at some easy tips:

0:30. Pay off as much debt as you can. Do this without dipping into the cash you'll need for your down payment, closing/settlement costs and an adequate emergency reserve fund.

0:26. Turn long-term debt (more than 10 months of payments left) into short-term debt. For instance, say you have 15 months left on a student loan. Make extra payments so you have only 10 or fewer months remaining by the time your credit score is reviewed.

0:22. Retire debt with the highest monthly payments first. Pay off the credit card that requires a $90 monthly payment before the one that only requires $50 per month.

0:18. Consolidate debt at a lower interest rate. Simply transfer the balance from a higher-rate credit card to one that has a lower interest rate. Remember, though, it's better to have two cards with balances each below 30% of the cards' credit limits than one card with a balance closer to the maximum allowed.

0:13. Minimize credit-card accounts to just four or five. Pay off store-issued cards first. When considering cards issued through major credit-card companies, such as VISA®, MasterCard® or American

BUDGET

Express®, pay off your newest accounts and those with the highest interest rates. Consider closing accounts only if you have too many — say, more than four or five — but you might be better off having zero balances on the remaining accounts than closing them.

0:09. Limit new inquiries into your credit as much as possible.
Don't get blindsided. Excessive inquiries by potential creditors (even if you aren't approved for credit) lower your credit score. Concentrate credit inquiries in a time frame that all relates to your mortgage application — say, 45 days before submitting.

0:04. Remedy any tax liens†† on your credit report. Pay them off or correct them if there is a mistake.

> ††*Liens*
> A lien is simply a constraint placed on the title of a property. Liens can be placed on a property by the IRS, creditors, homeowners associations, local taxing authorities, lenders, builders and contractors, along with former owners of the home or land and their heirs in order to recover money owed to them. A home can have multiple liens on it. *Smart Tip:* Avoid liens at all cost.

5 Ways To Sabotage Your Credit Score Without Knowing It

1. **Paying bills late.** Once you are 30 days late paying a bill, your credit score can drop, sometimes a significant 60 to 110 points. Not paying a bill at all has even worse consequences.

2. **Applying for or opening new credit accounts** can lower your credit score, so consider doing so carefully or avoid it altogether 120 days before your mortgage application. Don't open any new accounts once you have applied for a mortgage. *Smart Tip:* Although credit inquiries from lenders ("hard" inquiries) can lower your score, checking your credit report for accuracy ("soft" inquiry) will not affect your credit score.

3. **Closing credit-card accounts.** It's counter-intuitive, but having unused credit — that is, accounts with no balances — can actually help your credit score by reducing your debt-to-credit ratio. Certainly, you can have too many open credit accounts — more than six or so.

If you think you need to close some accounts, do so before applying for your mortgage.

4. **Having high balances on your credit accounts.** Keep balances on your credit-card accounts to less than 30% of your credit limits. Having $3,000 in balances spread over four accounts will be better for your credit score than having all $3,000 on one account.

5. **Making major purchases.** Using credit to buy a suite of furniture, a new car or kitchen appliances for the new home increases your debt-to-credit ratio — which lowers your score. Making a major purchase *after* applying for a mortgage changes your financial picture and could jeopardize loan approval.

3 STEPS TO CORRAL DOWN PAYMENT AND CLOSING CASH

It's no mystery: The key to a healthy body is diet and exercise. Like that, the key to healthy credit/debt is restraint and budgeting. Here's how:

1. Figure out how you really spend your money.

We get it: This is boring. But it's essential. Look back four to six months (a full year is even better) to track receipts and electronic transfers for every single purchase or payment you make. Then sort each expenditure into one of the following four categories: "must spend," "don't need but really value," "probably could live without" and "total waste of money." When you total each category, you'll get a surprising picture of how much room you have to reorient the way you use money.

2. Build a realistic spending plan.

🍽 **Start with your income.** Then subtract all the payments you must make each month. (It's smart to contribute monthly to a separate account to plan ahead for payments made quarterly or twice per year, such as insurance or taxes.)

🍽 **Request level billing for utilities,** with equal payments due each month. With this tip, you won't be ambushed by, say, a large electric bill in the middle of summer.

💬 **Set aside amounts for necessary monthly outlays.**
Think health care, transportation, clothing, education and so on.
(Look for ways to cut those costs and save money.) Calculate average
yearly maintenance/repair costs for your home and vehicle(s). Then
set aside one-twelfth of that amount in your separate account for
non-monthly expenses.

💬 **Build a contingency fund.** Do this as quickly as possible. Hands
off: Only tap your rainy-day fund in case of a dire emergency — such as
losing employment. How much you need to squirrel away will depend
on your financial situation. For Smarties who are relatively debt-free,
experts recommend socking away anywhere from three to six months or
more of monthly expenses. If you're trying to pay off debt, try to build a
fund that would cover at least a month or two of expenses.

💬 **Save for retirement.** Making retirement savings a necessary
monthly expense will help ensure that you have something to live on
when employment income stops. Plus your regular contributions over
the long term will multiply exponentially due to the eighth wonder of
the world: compound interest.

💬 **Pay off debts.** Money left over after budgeting for the above
priorities should first be applied to paying off outstanding debt,
especially credit cards and store accounts that charge hefty monthly
interest rates. Once you've cleared your accounts, you can divvy up the
remainder of your income for non-essential spending — recreation,
entertainment, vacations, investments, etc.

3. Use Creative Ways To Find Down Payment Cash (Besides In The Sofa) If you're having trouble saving for a down
payment and closing/settlement costs,
consider the following alternatives to boost
your cash stash:

💬 **Receive a tax-free gift from your parents** (or others)
documented by a "gift letter" stating no repayment is required (thus
your debt burden is not increased). Children can receive up to $13,000
from each parent in one year tax free. Run the math: That means a
couple can get gifts totaling up to $104,000 from four parents (or
grandparents) without any gift tax consequences ($13,000 x 4 x 2 =
$104,000). Better still, the folks can repeat the gift on January 1 (new
tax year). Some lenders may require you to use some of your own money
in addition to the gift.

● **Negotiate a secured loan or shared-equity arrangement** with parents or other people looking for a good investment. You can, if you like, buy them out later.

● **Sell something of value** (real estate, jewelry, collectibles, automobile, etc.), with the realization that you'll be able to replace it later.

● **Take a penalty-free early withdrawal** of up to $10,000 from an IRA for a down payment.

● **Finance the closing/settlement costs** by adding them to your loan amount, if your lender agrees, or get help from the seller.

● **Use the proceeds from an income tax refund.**

● **Borrow on your life insurance, company pension plan or securities.** If you own bonds, an IRA, vested pension or profit sharing, some banks will lend you cash against these as collateral. The portfolio must be negotiable, although not immediately available.

● **Use your business as collateral.**

● **Ask for a cash payment bonus** from your employer instead of a raise.

● **Obtain an advance** on a future inheritance. (Doesn't hurt to ask.)

SMART GUIDE TO GOOD DEBT VERSUS BAD DEBT

Remember: No matter what life stage you're in, debt will have an impact on how you live. Let your debt get out of control and it will take control of your choices. Keep debt under control and you'll have more and better choices available.

On the flip side, don't confuse debt with credit. It's hard to get through life these days without credit in some form or another. You know what we mean if you've ever tried to book a hotel room or rent a car without a credit card. Good luck! The fact is, having credit is good, and a good credit profile can open many doors for the smart consumer.

Having debt, on the other hand, can be good or bad, depending on what you accomplish with that debt and how much you have relative to your income. Bad debt hurts your credit and can slam the door shut on many of life's options — including homeownership.

Good debt multiplies the benefits. Use debt to get an education so you can get a higher-paying job. Use it to buy a car to transport you to that job. Use debt to invest in a home to live in and an asset that's likely to appreciate over the long term. In each of these examples, good debt helps you accomplish something that can pay you back—ideally, much more than the amount you borrowed and the interest you paid.

That said, even this kind of debt can morph into bad debt if you borrow beyond your means to repay. Bad debt occurs when people borrow to buy things they can't pay cash for and could easily live without. Think vacations, furniture, clothes, jewelry, gifts, dining out, entertainment, daily non-fat decaf mocha cappuccinos—you get the idea.

It's one thing to use credit cards, then pay off the full balances every billing cycle. That's fine, especially if you're earning frequent-flier miles or some other perk for using your card. It's dangerous, though, to make only the minimum payments due every month. You'll quickly witness account balances evolving into monsters.

HOW A CO-SIGNER CAN BE RED BULL FOR A BUYER'S FINANCES

When would-be home buyers lack the kind of credit profile to qualify for a mortgage on their own, asking someone else to co-sign the loan may be just what it takes to buy a home today.

Be sure your co-signer fully understands the obligation. A co-signer is guaranteeing the loan and will bear as much responsibility for it as you, the home buyer. For starters, if you default on the mortgage, your co-signer will have to make the payments or risk damaging his or her own credit rating. To add another aspect: Information about the loan will show up on the co-signer's credit report, even if it's paid on time, affecting how much he or she can borrow for a home or other loan type. The co-signer's name cannot be removed from the mortgage until it is paid in full by selling the property or by you qualifying for a new loan without the co-signer.

Put yourself in their shoes. Your co-signer will likely be more comfortable co-signing a loan for you if:

▶ You have enough income to support the payments and are responsible about meeting your financial obligations.

▶ Your co-signer has enough income to make payments or pay off the loan without damaging their ability to meet their own obligations or secure more credit should they need it.

▶ The lender agrees to notify the co-signer, in writing, if you miss a payment. This would give the co-signer time to step in and make payments without having to repay the loan in full.

▶ The co-signer receives copies of all paperwork associated with the mortgage.

6 EASY STEPS TO KNOW HOW MUCH HOME YOU CAN AFFORD

Nailing what price home you can afford to buy can be a pain in the neck. Imagine calling multiple lenders, shopping a range of loan programs, assembling a spreadsheet on various mortgage rates and reviewing your finances with several lending officers. Ouch!

Fortunately, there's an easier way: Use an online calculator. Here's what you'll need . . . and a few simple steps to figure it out for yourself: (1) Get the approximate monthly payment a lender is apt to approve for you; (2) convert that payment into a mortgage amount given a current interest rate. That amount, plus the amount of your down payment, gives you the price range of homes you are qualified to buy. Gurus call this exercise "pre-qualification."

Your income sets how much you can pay monthly. Obviously. Yet lower interest rates increase the amount a lender will let you borrow. Also, lenders offer a range of loan plans that further increase how much they will lend you for the same monthly payment. That monthly payment is called PITI.†† The good news: Lower rates and different loan plans can increase your buying power.

> **††*PITI***
>
> What is PITI? Principal, Interest, Taxes, Insurance. These are the four elements that make up the payment that comes out of your checking account each month. (Most home buyers set up an escrow account with the lender to handle payments for taxes and insurance along with the monthly principal and interest payment.) These costs are often called "carrying costs." Be careful when getting quotes on payments and find out whether the figure is the full PITI or just principal and interest (PI), which is much lower.

BUDGET

Remember, the price range of homes you can afford is figured after a down payment is added to your qualified loan amount. In addition, you'll need to set aside an amount for closing/settlement costs and points payments, if any. Here's where some buyers get tripped up. Although lenders qualify borrowers based on PITI, smart buyers also allocate income to meet maintenance, utility costs and any homeowners or condominium fees.

To keep things easy now, first look online to find what interest rate is currently being charged for 30-year fixed-rate loans (search words: current mortgage interest rates).

Now you can apply the following do-it-yourself system to zero in on the approximate mortgage amount lenders are likely to approve. Ready? Here goes:

1. **Find your "debt ratio."** Mortgage lenders want to ensure that you don't take on more debt than you can handle. They focus on the size of monthly payment (PITI) you can afford given your income and other long-term debts. The maximum allowed debt ratio varies by lender, loan program and size of down payment, but a common debt-ratio limit is 36%. Find your debt ratio as follows:

   ▶ **Calculate your gross monthly income** — the amount you make before deductions. Add your spouse's gross monthly income, if any, and any other income you receive monthly — child support, alimony, etc.

   ▶ **Multiply your gross monthly income by 36% (.36).** If your income is $5,000, the result would be $1,800. (That $1,800 represents your maximum debt-ratio amount for a lender using the 36% cap.)

   ▶ **Subtract long-term monthly debts** (more than 10 months to pay-off), such as car loan payments, personal loans, alimony, child support or regular payments toward a credit card balance. The result is the maximum housing payment many lenders would think you can afford. In our example, if your monthly long-term debts total $300, a lender using the 36% debt-ratio limit would approve you for monthly PITI payments of no more than $1,500. (Be warned: Some lenders and mortgage plans apply more or less strict factors, such as 33% with a 5% down payment or 38% with a 20% down payment.)

2. **Find your "housing ratio."** Lenders also apply a cap on the amount of your income that is only going toward a housing payment (again, PITI). This lower cap—often set at 28% of gross monthly income—does not take your long-term monthly debts into consideration. Going back to our example, if your gross monthly income is $5,000, a lender applying a 28% housing-ratio cap would approve you for a PITI payment of no more than $1,400 ($5,000 x .28 = $1,400).

Note: Most lenders will cap your PITI payment to the *lower* amount yielded by calculating the two ratios—in our example, that would be $1,400.

3. **Take a guesstimate of average annual real estate taxes for the home you want to buy, plus the annual cost of homeowners insurance.** Divide by 12 to obtain a monthly figure. On average, the monthly cost of these two items might be about one-tenth of 1% of the home's purchase price (multiply the purchase price by .001).

4. **Deduct the estimated monthly taxes and insurance costs from each of the figures you arrived at in Steps 2 and 3.** The result is the ballpark monthly payment for principal and interest (PI) you can afford to pay on a mortgage. Knowing the PI payment you can make and the current mortgage interest rate (ask a lender for a quote), you can find the mortgage loan amount you can afford. *Smart Tip:* To find a specific estimate for your situation, simply search online using the words "mortgage calculator." Be prepared to enter your figures, such as loan amount, down payment amount, loan type and interest rate.

◆ ◆ ◆

Essential Takeaway

Essential Takeaway: How much you earn versus how much you owe determines how much a lender will let you borrow. But a lender may let you borrow so much that you could get into trouble financially; how much a lender will lend and how much you can afford—or should borrow—are two different things. Avoid the temptation to be house-poor, borrowing the maximum a lender will lend (think housing bubble). Smart buyers keep their housing expenses within manageable limits. Be sure to allow for home-related expenses such as taxes, insurance, utilities, furniture, upkeep, housekeeping, lawn service, condo or HOA fees and improvements — not to mention other obligations for college tuition, medical expenses, etc. You'll also need a cushion for rising interest rates if you get an adjustable-rate loan plus property tax and insurance increases.

◆ ◆ ◆

HOW TAXES INCREASE BUYING POWER

Your home provides shelter for you and your taxes. The stunning fact is that homeownership is one of the most tax-favored investments most people make:

🗩 The interest paid on your loan is deductible, as are your property taxes. This interest deduction is also a major tax advantage in owning a second home.

🗩 You may deduct a portion of your home expenses if you have a qualifying home office.

🗩 Many health-related additions to your home required by your doctor (such as air conditioning for an asthma sufferer) are deductible, provided the addition does not add to the value of your home.

🗩 Casualty losses (such as flooding, hurricane damage, etc.) that are not reimbursed by insurance are deductible, subject to income limits.

It gets better: When it's time to sell your home, tax savings help defray many of the expenses of selling, such as:

🗩 A married couple can usually exclude from taxation up to $500,000 of capital gains realized on the sale of their principal residence ($250,000 for singles and married taxpayers filing separately).

🗩 If your gross gains are more than the $500,000 or $250,000 exclusion amounts, be aware that you can subtract the cost of home improvements from your net sales price. ("Net sales price" is your sale price minus closing costs, broker's and lawyer's fees.) You can also subtract title insurance fees, recording fees, transfer taxes and other acquisition costs. This reduces your gain and also your taxes.

🗩 You can reduce your immediate tax burden, in situations where the gain is larger than the exclusion amounts, by making an installment sale where you spread out your income — and taxes — over a period of years.

🔹 If, when you sell, you have to pay a lender's penalty for prepaying your mortgage, that charge can be deducted on your taxes. Fortunately, many mortgages do not have prepayment penalties today.

🔹 Under certain conditions, you may deduct moving expenses within limits.

Why Your Paycheck Gets Bigger When You Buy A Home

Did you know that home buying can increase your paycheck? You win, Smartie! Buying a home adds to your "take home" paycheck because you can max your withholding in anticipation of mortgage interest and other deductions on your next tax return. By increasing your allowances, you reduce the amount withheld to pay future taxes — which puts your tax refund in your paycheck today, not at the end of the year. This is true if you're renting now or if your new mortgage interest payments are higher than you now pay. Ask your tax preparer to estimate how many allowances you should claim to compensate for reduced taxes caused by your home-related interest deductions.

◆ ◆ ◆

Essential Takeaway

Essential Takeaway: Keep in mind that on both 15-year and 30-year loans, your interest deduction is highest in the first few years of the loan, so your tax deduction is highest then, too. If you pre-pay part of your loan with extra payments or additional principal pay-down, you also reduce your tax deduction. How long you plan to keep your loan can help determine which type of loan and which payment strategy is best for you.

◆ ◆ ◆

That's it for keeping Uncle Sam away. Now let's dive into how you can afford the home you want. We'll show you the money shortly in Chapter 4.

Chapter 3 Roundup

Smart Essentials BUDGET :: What You Have Learned

►► Nurture your credit like your first born.

►► 30-second course to power up your credit.

►► 5 ways to sabotage your credit score without knowing it.

►► Corral your down payment and closing cash.

►► Creative ways to find down payment cash
(besides in the sofa).

►► Smart guide to good debt versus bad debt.

►► How a co-signer can be Red Bull for buyers' finances.

►► Six easy steps to know how much home you can afford.

►► How taxes increase buyer power.

►► Why your paycheck gets bigger when you buy a home.

Smart Essentials

Page	Essential Note

CHAPTER 4
MONEY

In this chapter, you'll learn smart ways to:

1. Know how to separate the right loan from the wrong one in your situation.

2. Ask your lender smart questions to avoid overpaying for your loan.

3. Avoid costly pitfalls that can cause lender rejection.

SELECT THE RIGHT LOAN FOR YOUR SPECIFIC SITUATION

Like ABBA sings: "Money, money, money . . . Must be sunny . . . In the rich man's world." How to get a little of the rich man's money is the point of this chapter. Hot tip: Not all mortgage money is created the same.

Before you get up-close and personal with the costs of a mortgage, you first must select a loan plan designed to meet your needs. Maximize your buying power? Minimize monthly payment? What plan works best with the down payment cash you have? All of the above? Now for a crash course in mortgage-loan basics:

Adjustable-rate mortgage (ARM). The initial interest rate on an ARM is lower than a conventional loan, thereby resulting in lower monthly payments. The rate rises or falls at intervals, but within limits. Ask about five-year or seven-year options offering no rate adjustment until the fifth or seventh year, then annual adjustments after that. Desirable ARMs have below-market rates for the first period, then limits ("caps") on how much rates can adjust (ideal: 2% to 3% max increase per adjustment; 5% to 6% life-of-loan increase). Compare several lenders for the best terms.

Fixed rates. If you're more comfortable with the security of a higher-priced fixed-rate loan, opting for a longer term (30 years rather than 15 years) may put monthly payments within reach. Although you would pay more in interest over the life of the loan, most homeowners plan to move before 30 years are up. You get peace of mind that your loan payments will not increase.

● **VA guaranteed loan.** If you are an eligible veteran, the Department of Veterans Affairs requires no down payment (up to a specific sales price) for a VA-insured mortgage.

● **FHA-insured loan.** Insured by the Federal Housing Administration, your loan (obtained through an approved, qualified lender) requires a lower down payment and interest rate than most other mortgages. The minimum down payment for an FHA-insured loan is usually 3.5% of the purchase price. In some areas of the country, down-payment requirements may be even lower for qualified borrowers.

● **FHA 203(k) rehab loan.** Lenders offer this government-backed home-improvement loan to purchase or rehab a home with a mortgage that covers the costs in one loan. These loans are especially popular for buying distressed properties that need fix-up. The pre-approved repair work must increase the home's value to justify the additional upfront loan amount. Expect extra paperwork, such as contractor bids, before- and after-work appraisals, escrow accounts, holdbacks, inspections, etc.

● **Seller take-back.** Some sellers are willing to consider seller financing (in several formats) designed to reduce buyers' payments. One format is a short-term second mortgage secured by the home and accepted by the seller to help trim the buyer's down-payment requirements. Another is a long-term first mortgage, but without the usual qualification standards.

● **Mortgage assumption.** When you assume an existing loan, your down payment is the difference between the home's sale price and the loan balance. By finding an assumption with a high unpaid balance, you may reduce your down payment. If the loan has a lower-than-market interest rate, you'll also reduce your monthly payments. In most cases, the seller's lender must approve the loan assumption.

● **Co-signed loan.** A co-signer's credit helps you qualify for a larger loan over a longer term, making monthly payments smaller than you would otherwise qualify for because the co-signer is on the hook to make payments should you default.

● **Shared equity.** This is a situation in which you buy your home with a parent, relative, friend or other qualified investor who makes the down payment. You share the purchase costs, the maintenance, the monthly payments—and equity profits on sale.

💬 **All cash.** Paying all cash and not using other people's money (OPM) is an option. All cash, or "hard money," is not uncommon for investors, second-home and move-up buyers with equity to transfer to their next home. Also using cash, sometimes, are wealthy buyers (or their heirs) and buyers who've proven their luck by winning a lottery.

💬 **Jumbo loan.** This is a loan size, rather than a type. Jumbos exceed the limit for "conforming" loans and carry higher rates. That limit varies by area and is periodically revised by the two federally chartered organizations, Fannie Mae and Freddie Mac. These two semi-private corporations purchase loans from originating banks and lenders, bundle similar loans and resell the packages as securities to investors. This secondary market replenishes lenders' funds so they can make more loans. Ask your lender for the current conforming/jumbo limits in your area.

◆ ◆ ◆

Essential Takeaway

Essential Takeaway: *Financing a home purchase is a critical — and complex — subject for every home buyer. What you know about mortgage plans, rates, points, lock-ins, taxes, even selecting a lender, can literally save you — or cost you — thousands of dollars. Different buyers have different mortgage needs. Be sure to get a top loan officer on your team to find and put numbers to the many mortgage options available on the street today. The more you know about financing, the better your decisions will be at every step in the process.*

◆ ◆ ◆

9 MUST-ASK QUESTIONS TO PICK A WINNER LOAN

Finding a low interest rate on a mortgage is important, but lenders package loans in various ways that can make a big difference over the life of your loan. To pick a winner loan, consider these essential issues about the full mortgage package you are buying. The answers could save — or cost — a bundle.

1. Rates? What rates are available today on the loan programs you are interested in? Remember, the lowest interest rate is not necessarily the best loan. Additional fees and costs can sometimes increase your loan expenses considerably. That's why comparing the annual percentage rate[††]—which includes many costs such as interest rate, origination fee, points and most loan fees—is important.

> ### [††]*Annual Percentage Rate (APR)*
>
> The APR provides a common denominator you can use to compare loans side by side, just like gas mileage lets you compare cars. APR can be confusing at first because it's always higher than the nominal interest rate quoted by the lender. That's because APR includes what you are really paying annually over the life of the loan. Lenders must disclose both the nominal interest rate and the APR on the Good Faith Estimate they're required to give you when you apply for a loan.
>
> As an example (current rates will vary), one lender may offer a 30-year mortgage for $100,000 at 6% with 1 discount point, $1,000 in fees and an APR of 6.186%. Compare that to another loan at 5.75% with 2 points, $1,500 in fees and an APR of 6.024%. The APR of the second loan looks like a better deal. And it would be, provided the borrower owns the home long enough for monthly-payment savings to recoup higher upfront costs.
>
> The second loan would save the borrower $15.98 in monthly principal/interest payments. However, the borrower would have to own the home for almost 94 months (about 7.8 years) before savings break even with the higher cost of fees and points ($1,500/$15.98 = 93.87 months). A borrower who plans to sell sooner than 94 months would save money taking the first loan with the higher interest rate and APR but with lower upfront costs.
>
> *Smart Tip:* APR *does not* account for costs such as title insurance premiums, non-refundable application fees, fees for appraisals, document preparation fees or title examination costs.

2. **Terms?** Loan term is the length of time to repay a loan (30 years, 15 years, etc.). ("Terms" is also a word used to define the specifics of a loan program.) For an adjustable-rate mortgage (ARM), terms include: rate adjustment period, frequency of monthly payment adjustments, possible extension of the length of time on the loan pay-off, as well as a maximum limit on each rate change, ceiling on payment adjustments, life-of-the-loan interest-rate cap, conversion privilege to fixed rate, positive or negative amortization, etc.

3. **Points?** A loan with a low interest rate and many points costs thousands of dollars more up front than a higher-rate loan with fewer points. (One point equals 1% of the loan amount.) Yet a lower rate means a lower monthly payment. Remember: Discount points — essentially pre-paid mortgage interest — are deductible on your income taxes in the year of purchase.

4. **Fees?** Some lenders quote very low interest rates and points, and then charge higher fees. Ask for a list of upfront and closing fees and what they cover. It's smart to have everything on the table — in writing from the beginning — so there are no misunderstandings later.

Of course, as required by law your lender will give you a "Good Faith Estimate" (GFE) of all settlement costs within three days of your loan application. That estimate probably ranges from as low as 1% of the loan amount up to perhaps 8% depending on multiple factors: the lender, whether you're paying points to get a lower interest rate, the home you're purchasing and its location, your down payment amount, the day and month you close, as well as other factors. Typically, however, buyer's closing costs average around 3% of the loan amount. When you get your GFE, examine the estimate and ask for an explanation of fees.

5. **Requirements?** Lenders talk about down-payment and loan requirements as a percentage of the home's value, such as a 20% down or 80% loan-to-value (LTV[††]). They also mandate what type(s) of insurance will you need to purchase a home — basic homeowners, flood, etc. You'll also want to know what inspections are required for the home you select.

[††] *LTV*
A loan-to-value (LTV) ratio expresses the difference between what a lender will lend toward the purchase of a home and the market value of a home. For example, if the home is

worth $100,000 and the lender agrees to a loan of $80,000, the LTV would be 80% ($80,000 ÷ $100,000 = .80 or 80%). The borrower fills the gap (20%) using a combination of down payment, other loans secured by the home (e.g., a second mortgage) or, if refinancing, equity held in the home. Borrowers with better credit can get higher LTV loans — for example, 85% or 90% or 95% — because they present less risk to the lender. You can also get a higher LTV loan by purchasing private mortgage insurance (PMI).

6. Lock-In? Ask about the procedures to lock-in[††] an attractive rate for a specified time. There may be a lock-in fee, sometimes up to 1% of the loan amount. Be sure your lock-in is in writing and includes both the rate and points, because either one can change. If rates and points are rising, the one-time lock-in fee at application could save you money at settlement and over the life of a loan.

> [††] ***Lock-In***
> Lock-ins minimize risk when interest rates rise. Although today's mortgage interest rates may still be very attractive, there's no telling how long they will stay that way. When interest rates rise, they can move suddenly. When they do, even a half-point increase can increase your costs and dramatically reduce your buying power. If rates rise, you are guaranteed the rate and points you initially agreed to with the lock-in. (Note: Rate locks expire, often in 45 or 60 days.) *Smart Tip:* Avoid the drag of losing your rate lock because of slow loan approval by responding quickly to every lender request.

7. Processing? If time is of the essence, you will want a quick processing and funding turnaround time. Providing your lender with a complete application can speed up this process. Ask how long the lender has been taking to approve loans lately.

8. PMI? If you can't afford a 20% down payment, you may need private mortgage insurance (PMI)[††] to cover the lender's risk should you default on the loan. Traditional PMI involves a monthly premium payment that will end automatically once you have paid 22% of the loan balance. There are also single-premium, pay-upfront plans that can reduce your monthly payment.

††*Private Mortgage Insurance (PMI)*

PMI allows home buyers to sidestep the 20% down payment most mortgage lenders require. (BTW, government-backed loans, such as FHA, call this fee a mortgage insurance premium [MIP]. Same animal, different name.) If you have enough income to support a monthly mortgage payment but too little cash for a 20% down payment, PMI helps you buy now. Downside: PMI increases your monthly payment. Ask your lender for current PMI costs.

On the flip side: PMI is automatically cancelled once your loan-to-value ratio reaches 78% or less — that is, you've paid off 22% of the original loan amount. Also, lenders must terminate PMI coverage once the loan reaches the midpoint of the amortization schedule, for example, at month 180 on a 360-month (30-year) loan term. You also have the right to *request* PMI termination once your mortgage balance is paid down to 80% of the home's original purchase price or the appraised value at time of purchase — whichever is lower. Finally, you can ask your lender to cancel PMI based on proof that your LTV has declined to 80% or less of current value, either through appreciation or improvements.(Chances are you'll have to pay for an appraisal to prove your home's increased value.)

9. **Prepayment?** If you decide to pay off your loan early, is there a prepayment penalty? Some homeowners decide to make additional payments to pay off their mortgage more quickly, but this method can incur a penalty with some loan programs. And if you have a low interest rate, you might be better off investing the extra cash elsewhere, anyway.

SMART HOME BUYERS GET MORTGAGE PRE-APPROVAL FIRST

Shopping for a home before you're pre-qualified for a loan is putting the cart before the horse. Bidding to buy a home before you're *pre-approved* for a mortgage is shooting your offer in the foot. Ignoring the mixed metaphors, Smarties are most successful buying today when they have "cash in their pocket" with a loan pre-approval. Why?

● **Pre-qualification.** Pre-qualification is simply a verbal exchange in which the lender looks at what you say is your income and debt and estimates how much you could afford to spend on a mortgage. Once you have a rough idea of how much you can afford, it's a lot easier to home shop online (qualified loan amount + down payment = affordable price range). While writing a purchase offer with pre-qualification is better than doing so without, sellers may not want to pin their sale on your chances of getting a loan. If a lender finds inaccuracies or problems in your credit that even you didn't know about, then settlement could be delayed or even canceled altogether. That's why sellers prefer *pre-approved* buyers.

● **Pre-approval.** For you to be pre-approved, your lender requires a full application and will verify all the information on the loan app. Loan pre-approval is a commitment from a lender to provide you with a loan for a specified amount — assuming the home chosen meets the lender's requirements and your financial picture doesn't change before settling/closing on the home. Pre-approval means everything you put on the application has been verified: income, employment, debts, credit history and more. When you're pre-approved for a loan, sellers have peace of mind knowing that financing problems will not ruin the deal at the last minute. Quite simply: Your offer looks better to a seller compared with buyers who don't know if they can get a loan.

| **More Mortgage Lingo Made Simple** | Lenders use ratios as a kind of shorthand. We've talked about this before, but debt-to-income is a critical ratio every buyer must know. |

Debt-to-income ratio is the relationship of a borrower's monthly payment obligation on long-term debts divided by gross monthly income, expressed as a percentage. A common set of ratios used by mortgage lenders is 28/36. The "front end" ratio indicates that no more than 28% of a buyer's gross income can be used for the mortgage payment (PITI). The "back end" ratio limits PITI combined with all other long-term monthly debt payments to no more than 36% of gross income. Ask your lender what debt ratios they use to judge your application.

6 MUST-DO'S TO AVOID LENDER REJECTION

Qualifying for a mortgage was easier just a few years ago. But remember: Today's tighter lending standards help ensure that borrowers have the financial ability to keep the homes they buy as long as they want to. When applying for a mortgage today, here are several must-do's to ensure you don't jeopardize your loan application.

1. **Boost your credit score to 740 or higher.** Though loans are available to borrowers with lower scores, with a FICO score of 740 or higher you'll get the best interest rates and lowest downpayment requirement.

2. **Prove your income.** Lenders like to see consistent income over a period of two to five years. Of course, you'll also need enough predictable income to handle your monthly loan payment, property taxes and insurance.

3. **Flash the cash.** The more down payment you invest in your home, the better risk you are considered by lenders. Lenders consider a 20% to 30% down payment ideal, with a solid emergency fund of four to six times monthly income backing that up. You may get a loan with less, but why not go for the gold?

4. **Minimize debt.** Pay down credit cards and retire car loans, student-loan debt, etc. to improve your debt-to-income ratio, leaving more room in your budget for mortgage debt.

5. **Tell the truth.** Your loan-application information will be verified through the underwriting process. Remember, incomplete or false disclosures will simply derail lender confidence in you.

6. **Avoid last-minute gaffes.** Lenders will calculate your debt-to-income ratio at the beginning of the loan process. They'll also pull your credit report just before settlement. Don't change the picture by depleting cash resources, increasing debt or opening new credit accounts.

Why Does It Take So Long To Approve A Loan? Typically, the lender will give or send you an application "package" with instructions and necessary forms. You complete these in detail, including the financial data and account numbers. Most lenders require a loan application fee to cover a credit report and appraisal.

A lender takes several steps in processing your application, and different procedures exist in different areas. Primarily, your lender is busy doing the following:

💬 Getting an appraisal of the home you want to buy, to assure the lender it's worth the price you are paying.

💬 Getting reports on your employment, income and debt-paying ability, to determine if you are a good credit risk. A form is sent to your employer to confirm your position and income. For self-employed applicants, lenders take a look at tax returns and profit/loss statements. Verifying your credit tells your lender about your current and past credit accounts, balances, payment habits, foreclosures, judgments, etc.

💬 Verifying bank deposits to satisfy down payment and closing cost needs. Your financial institutions also receive forms to confirm you have enough money in reserves to pay for closing costs, down payment and other purchasing expenses.

💬 Ordering inspections, such as housing or building code compliance, completion of repairs the seller agreed to make, termites or other wood-boring insects.

💬 Ordering the title search (sometimes by the lender's lawyer or a title insurance company) to determine if the seller can convey clear title to you.

💬 Verifying hazard (homeowners) insurance coverage, to make sure the home is protected against major losses.

Once all the documents are assembled, a review of your application by the lender's loan committee determines whether or not your loan is approved. When your application is approved, your lender sends you a loan confirmation letter to put the loan amount, interest rate and monthly payment in writing.

◆ ◆ ◆

Essential Takeaway

Essential Takeaway: Here is where your buyer's agent's knowledge of what your lender needs—and where the information comes from—can help prod the process along, even if it means carrying papers from one place to another. The process works best when you rely on a real estate agent, and lenders appreciate the agent as a single source to turn to for answers. It's also smart to prod your agent to confirm different sources of information and needed action: Has your bank supplied your account information? Have your credit-card companies produced reports? Will your insurance policy be guaranteed to be in effect by settlement or closing day? Have your parents, relatives or friends provided the "gift letter" that must accompany cash gifts? Has your employer verified your income, etc.?

❖ ❖ ❖

Are we there yet? Closer, but no cigar. By now you have a pretty good idea where your money is coming from. But what will it buy? In Chapter 5, we get to the fun part . . . actually shopping for the neighborhood and perfect home that will be your new home sooner than you think. Let the games begin!

Chapter 4 Roundup

Smart Essentials MONEY :: What You Have Learned

▶▶ How to select the right loan for your specific situation.
▶▶ 9 must-ask questions to pick a winner loan.
▶▶ Smart home buyers get mortgage pre-approval first.
▶▶ 6 must-do's to avoid lender rejection.
▶▶ Why it takes so long to approve a loan.

Smart Essentials

Page	Essential Note

CHAPTER 5

SHOP

In this chapter, you'll learn smart ways to:

1. Learn the right way to size up a neighborhood.

2. Inspect a home like a bloodhound and spot a money pit before it's too late.

3. Avoid little-known and very costly home shopping mistakes.

7 CARDINAL RULES FOR TODAY'S BUYERS TO SELL SMART TOMORROW

An old real estate maxim says, "The best time to think about selling your home is when you're buying it." That's because location will be a prime factor influencing future buyers when it comes time to sell your home. Bottom line: It pays to keep resale value in mind from the start.

1. **Look for a strong, diversified local economy.** Employment from business expansions and new companies moving to an area mean more home buyers. That increased demand can help home prices rise.

2. **Consider areas with lowest (or no) taxes** including state income tax, personal property tax, etc. These areas attract buyers.

3. **Check out local school ratings.** Property values track closely with the quality of schools and the level of local funding.

4. **Look for low-crime areas** and active neighborhood watch programs.

5. **Check local zoning laws** and plans for development to find out if the area could change for the better or the worse.

6. **Research how fast homes sell.** Learn how often homes in the neighborhood are listed for sale and how quickly they sell. The fewer that list and the faster they sell, the more demand there is for the neighborhood.

7. **Buy a modest home in a top neighborhood** rather than a top home in a modest neighborhood. You want your home's value to look like a bargain compared to your neighbors' homes.

SHOP

HOW TO SIZE UP NEW LOCATIONS FROM A DISTANCE

Some communities speak loud and clear at first glance; the quality of life is apparent in their streets, parks, buildings, homes and yards. You get a feel for them (either for or against) just by looking.

With a little online investigation, along with a few questions to your buyer's agent, you can fill in community details that aren't so obvious at first glance. These include:

- ▶ Location of schools, supermarkets, libraries, hospitals, places of worship, fire and police stations.
- ▶ Applicable zoning regulations.
- ▶ Available community services.
- ▶ What construction plans are in the offing.
- ▶ Planned shifts in transportation facilities.
- ▶ Whether home values have appreciated or depreciated.
- ▶ Prevailing tax rates.

Inspecting a community is as necessary as inspecting the home you want to buy. For a more intimate impression, walk around every community that looks attractive to you. Don't forget to take photos as you tour different locales. The online app *http://www.Pinterest.com* is a fun way to store your findings until later, when you'll want to separate different streets, homes and prices in your mind.

Smart Ways To Look Under The Hood Of A Prospective 'Hood

What is the neighborhood like? That's an excellent question that you need to ask. And where do you get the best answers? From neighbors in the homes near where you're thinking of buying a home. Whether your would-be neighbors are friendly or stand-offish, welcoming or distant, it's best to know this before you move in.

1. **Take a tour.** Drive through your prospective neighborhood on a weekday, on a weekend day and at night. Compare how it feels to what you expect it to feel like. Do you feel comfortable and safe? Will your family and guests feel comfortable and safe?

2. **Property status.** First, eyeball the area. How do the lawns and landscaping look? How do the other homes on the block look in terms of upkeep? Visible evidence of neglected maintenance include excessively tall grass, overgrown flower beds, peeling paint, broken windows or doors, etc. If these sights bother you, it's going to affect the perceptions of other buyers when it comes time for you to sell the home. Pride of ownership should be evident in the area where you want to buy. Having pride in one's home includes keeping it up and maintaining its appearance — and value.

3. **People.** It's best if you can talk in-person with your immediate prospective neighbors. First impressions are important, and they're as curious about new neighbors as you are. Ask them important questions about the neighborhood, as well as the home you're considering. Let the neighbors do the talking, and you'll learn a lot.

4. **Pets.** Do your immediate neighbors have dogs or other pets? Where are they housed at night, and when are they let outside? Are they fenced securely? Do the pets look well cared for? If you're not interested in being disturbed by barking, you might reconsider your home choice. Good pet owners are courteous to their neighbors and take good care of their animals.

5. **Crime.** Before you sign on the dotted line to buy a home, be sure to check crime statistics for the area and also its address on any number of government websites to check if there are any known criminal offenders living in close proximity. Consider your safety, comfort and, later, your home's resale value should you discover individuals with serious criminal records living close by.

6. **Development.** Take a trip to the municipal center to find out about nearby development plans, rezoning, road construction, new construction, etc. It's beneficial to see what's on the books around your area and what you might welcome or not want to be living in the midst of.

7. **Vacancies.** Due to the many foreclosures that have occurred throughout the country, it's also a good idea to look over the homes in your new neighborhood to identify if any are vacant. If they are vacant, ask who is taking care of them and how long they have been empty. You might be dissuaded from an area that isn't as populated as it once was.

8. Traffic. Does your would-be home sit on a busy street or near busy transportation hubs? Travel it at different times of day to get a sense of the amount of traffic that passes by and if there are rush-hour bottlenecks. Take a listen at morning, noon and night to see if noise levels are bearable. Note parking for yourself and guests. Ask if local ordinances restrict the number of vehicles or parking of RVs, boats and trailers. If what you learn is a bummer, consider another home.

9. Kids. If you have kids, or expect to have children someday, you may want a kid-friendly neighborhood. How close are parks, playgrounds and schools? Are there many kids out playing who might be the age of your child(ren)? Approach parents you see in the area and ask what they like or dislike about the neighborhood.

10. Research. Ask about your neighborhood homeowners association (HOA), get a copy of its latest newsletter and visit the HOA website to learn about the big issues of the community. Locate the local newspaper online and read current editions, as well as some past issues, to get a feel for the concerns in the area.

Research Resources Every Home Buyer Can Tap

● **MLS.** The primary source of home-sale information comes from the local multiple listing service (MLS). Member real estate brokers throughout your area enter properties for sale into the MLS. The database of information and photos is fed to area brokerages and national websites. Today, everyone has access to the constantly updated information. Your buyer's agent also has special access to search housing information in formats only available to MLS members, such as recent comparable sales.

● **Online.** Numerous websites aggregate home-sale information. Some of the largest include *http://www.Zillow.com, http://www.Trulia.com, http://www.Realtor.com,* local brokerage websites and national real estate franchise websites. Even search engines make it easy with search terms such as "real estate in [geographic area]" on sites like *http://www.Google.com, http://www.Bing.com, http://www.Yahoo.com* and many more.

● **Tax Database.** Another source is your local real estate tax-assessment database. Many counties and cities now operate tax databases you can view online. Some databases are more accurate and up-to-date than others. You'll find parameters such as street address, parcel number, owner's name, etc.; plus record of property transfers with sale dates, prices, sellers/buyers names (you can see what the seller originally paid); property profile with construction type, square footage, number/type of rooms, baths, date built, amenities, lot size, condition, utilities, zoning type, etc. You'll also see assessed value for land and building/improvements (gives you a ballpark idea of value if you know on average how much market value is higher than tax-assessed value); neighborhood sales, sometimes with dates, prices, type of sales (here you can learn what nearby properties recently sold for and if any foreclosures impacted area prices).

🗩 **Buyer's Agent.** Hands down, a top-notch buyer's agent will be an invaluable source of information about areas, neighborhoods, homes and prices. Be aware that federal and state fair housing laws prohibit discriminating against or in favor of people because of their race, color, religion, national origin, age (40 or over), sex, familial status, disability or veteran status. Local ordinances may also apply, such as sexual orientation, immigration status, genetic information, etc. You'll be on safest ground to talk about the property, not the people.

❖ ❖ ❖

Essential Takeaway

Essential Takeaway: "You get what you pay for" applies to homes just as it does to other things. But most of us can't afford to buy the home that "has it all." You can help ensure the long-term value of your home investment by, at the very least, purchasing the value-increasing features you won't be able to add later on — location, view, architectural style, proximity to local amenities, etc. Once you move into your home, you can start adding other sought-after features as your budget allows.

❖ ❖ ❖

5 MUST-KNOW TIPS BEFORE YOU START HOUSE HUNTING

Some buyers are easily swayed by emotion when making the largest purchase of their lives. Avoid this costly gotcha. Keep your thinking cap on and develop a clear outline of what is important to you and your family (and your financial planner). A little homework now will give you a home you can live with for a long time.

After settling on the must-have, would-be-nice and can-live-without aspects of the home you're looking for, you're ready to go house shopping. You may find, along the way, that your "wish list" and "must haves" change. To avoid taxing your will power, write down your important items on a piece of paper, document or your smart phone. Make sure everyone in your family is also on the same page. Some Smarties say it helps to read lists out loud as they discuss homes they've previewed. Sharing your list with your buyer's agent will also help you stay on track as you trek through your top-choice homes.

Here are five insider tips you should know before you start house hunting:

1. **Curb appeal.** The house looks great at the curb and even better when you walk inside. That is great news. The house is likely in move-in condition — and probably has other home buyers seriously considering it. Remember, the "perfect" home can lead to a costly bidding war with other interested buyers. Before you put in a purchase offer, consult with your family and financial adviser and set a price ceiling above which you will not go — no matter what. Your buyer's agent can help you stick to that price point and negotiate for the best price.

2. **Status.** The house you are smitten with has a grand entry, large foyer, huge entertaining areas, great upgrades. You think, "My family will love this!" or "I can't wait to have our friends over for dinner!" Consider, though, if you are buying a home with the thought that it will impress others, does this home also truly match your housing needs and wants? You are the one paying the mortgage and living with the financial responsibility. Beware of overspending to keep up with "the Joneses." Ensure you're purchasing a beautiful home in an area where you'll find friendly neighbors, good schools and conveniences you need. On the flip side, it pays to squint past cosmetic eyesores that have turned off other buyers to see the solid bones of a great house.

3. **Competition.** You put in an offer on a home, and so did someone else. The seller counters your offer with a higher price. Sometimes in the heat of the battle — that is, a bidding war — the competition can change your perception and make you lose sight of your goals. Refer back to your maximum price amount regularly and don't try to "win" the house if it means paying more than you want to. Despite your emotions telling you otherwise, there are other "perfect" homes out there waiting for you if one gets away. Your pocketbook will thank you later. Stick within your financial limits when buying a home and negotiate so that you get the best deal that works for you.

4. **Overvaluing.** You will come to learn which homes are overpriced — and undervalued — when you tour enough properties in person and online. The trick is not talking yourself into believing an overpriced home is worth it. It may have all the features you're looking for, the right location, the right schools, etc. However, if the seller accepts your foolishly high offer for an overpriced home (what seller wouldn't?), it's not necessarily smooth sailing to closing/settlement. Your lender may not approve the mortgage if the appraisal comes in lower than the agreed-upon sales price. Ouch. A low appraisal can derail the purchase entirely. Rely on your buyer's agent to help you evaluate homes for sale and see which ones are priced correctly.

5. **Deadlines.** If you have a strict deadline for when you need to be in your new home, you might be setting yourself up for disappointment. If a career change, arrival of a new baby, job promotion or other big event is looming, your emotions might not be entirely focused on making a wise home purchase. Step back for a moment and clearly separate the life-changing event from the "other" life-changing event of purchasing a home. You don't want to feel pressured to "settle" for a home just to get that task checked off your list.

TAKE A CLOSER LOOK WITH A DO-IT-YOURSELF PRE-INSPECTION

Wondering what to look for in a home outside of peeking in closets and opening up a few cabinet doors? Here's a smart guide to important home elements you can inspect yourself.

Crawl the walls. Use a systematic approach to checking each and every wall. A good strategy would be to start to the left of the front door, then move to the right and keep moving in that direction room by room. Follow the same strategy on every floor. As you check the walls, look for settlement cracks, separating joints, defective plaster or other signs of stress or damage. Check wallpapered areas for crinkling or gathering, which may mean walls are settling or shifting. Watch for recent redecorating, repairs or remodeling that could be hiding a problem. Do the air vents look clean? Don't forget — before leaving each room, check the entire ceiling.

● **Look for leaks.** Loose or wrinkled wallpaper could indicate a water leak somewhere. Look for water stains on the ceiling and walls, in cabinets and under sinks. Use a flashlight to ensure you see everything. Spend time in the bathrooms, kitchen and in every area with pipes, checking for leaks and drips. Also, run the shower and basin, then flush the toilet to check water pressure. If the toilet appears to be the original, turn the tank cover over to find the manufacture date. Look for cracked or loose tiles and missing grout or mildew stains on the walls or floor, which could indicate a behind-the-wall leak. Check in the basement/crawl space for evidence of water or moisture. Locate the sump pump.

● **Plug into the electrical system.** Look for extension cords and multiple plugs in sockets, which could mean insufficient or poorly placed sockets. Are outlets near water sources equipped with GFCI (ground fault circuit interrupter) receptacles? Also, check every appliance to be sure it works well. Don't forget to inspect the utility bills for the last 12 months or more, if available. Check the furnace and A/C units, if applicable. Do they look clean and well kept? Are the filters clean? Where is the thermostat located, and is it programmable or an older style? Look up for smoke detectors and if there is a CO/2 detector.

● **Focus on condition.** Open and close every door and window. Look and listen for squeaking, sticking or a tendency to close on its own. Are any panes of glass clouded or cracked? Do wood frames look sturdy? Check for evidence of shifting or settling around the front stoop, chimney and walks, foundation, walls and places where the driveway, retaining walls and fence meet the house. Look for rotted wood around window and door frames and the condition/age of the caulk around all seals on the outside of the house. Also, check the deck for sturdiness. Go into the garage and check the walls, floors and doors — inside and out. While there, check the garage door opener and tracks for smooth operation. Has the driveway been sealed recently, and what is the condition of the concrete/brickwork?

● **Pay attention to pests.** Look for signs of termites, ants and other pests. Especially look along the foundation, around doors and entry points of wiring and pipes. Ensure there is a clearance of six inches or more between the mulch and siding and that no wood (firewood or landscaping timbers) is in contact with the home. Check the gutters, soffits, downspouts and grading of the yard to be sure water runs away from the home. Binoculars could prove useful for checking the condition of gutters and roof shingles. Are trees, roots and bushes trimmed back from the home?

● **Move up to the pros.** If everything looks good to you and you decide to purchase the home, consider a home inspection by a professional inspector before settlement or closing. In addition to the items you've inspected, your professional will also carefully inspect the major systems — roof, electrical, gas, plumbing and heating/air conditioning. The inspector can also check in the attic, basement and crawl space for proper ventilation and condition. Make arrangements to accompany the inspector, if you can, to ask questions along the way. Insist on a written report from the inspector detailing what the problems are with the home and how important each one is. You may want to consult a contractor to estimate repair costs on any problems found. *Smart Tip:* A professional home inspector will reveal if your home has expensive problems that need attention. Be aware that the seven most costly home defects to repair include foundation, roof, heating/cooling, pests/termites, mold, electrical wiring and plumbing. Just remember: Everything can be fixed — for a price.

◆ ◆ ◆

Essential Takeaway

Essential Takeaway: *We all have to live somewhere. Putting your housing budget to work with a home investment — rather than throwing it away on rent — makes good sense for most people in most markets. Although there's no guarantee a particular home will appreciate year after year, home buyers spend part of their monthly payments buying an asset they can eventually sell. The remainder of their monthly outlay pays interest to their lender, which is fully tax-deductible in most cases. Not only can you live in the home while it helps your wealth grow, your own home offers pride of ownership and a secure sense of place in your community.*

◆ ◆ ◆

| Avoid This Costly Home Finding Mistake: | **Forgetting to mention your buyer's agent when you sign in to open houses.** Your buyer's agent won't be able to tour every single home with you. |

But, if you visit an open house or a new home community and start talking to the seller's agent or builder's on-site rep and negotiating the purchase of the home without your buyer's agent, it's likely that your buyer's agent may not be able to step in later to negotiate for your best interests.

Solution: Once you have started working with a buyer's agent, you can continue to look at homes. Remember: Your buyer's agent is working on your behalf. You want your agent to be a part of the transaction, whether you find the home or they do. Listing agents representing sellers and builder's agents, while required to treat buyers honestly, are compelled to negotiate the best deal for their client—the seller or builder. Purchasing a house without a buyer's agent is like going to court without your lawyer.

Now what? The area checks out. The 'hood checks out. The home checks out. Can you feel your pulse racing? The time has come to make an offer. But just exactly *how* do you do that? Stay tuned. You'll learn plenty about crafting a purchase offer and negotiating like a riverboat gambler in Chapter 6.

Chapter 5 Roundup

Smart Essentials SHOP :: What You Have Learned

►► 7 cardinal rules for buyers today to sell smart tomorrow.
►► How to size up new locations from a distance.
►► Smart ways to look under the hood of a prospective 'hood.
►► Research resources every home buyer can tap.
►► 5 must-know tips before you start house hunting.
►► Take a closer look with a do-it-yourself pre-inspection.
►► Avoid the mistake of not mentioning your buyer's agent.

CHAPTER 6

NEGOTIATE

In this chapter, you'll learn smart ways to:

1. Offer the price to drive a bargain for the home of your dreams.

2. Counteroffer like a pro to get a great deal.

3. Use contract terms to get agreement and avoid costly negotiating mistakes.

HOW TO CRAFT AN IRRESISTIBLE PURCHASE OFFER

Once you've found the home you've been looking for, it's time to sit down and write up an offer to purchase. Why is this important? The terms and conditions of this document with approved counteroffers will become your sales contract. In every area, contracts to purchase vary depending on local laws and custom, as well as the situation.

Key Components Typical matters you and a seller may negotiate and agree on include price, amount of your deposit, etc. However, be sure to include all items that will convey with the house such as window coverings, appliances, swing set, etc. Don't forget to include all contingencies that must take place before settlement/closing including, but not limited to, the sale of your current home; inspections (pests, radon, mold, etc.); proof of clear title to the home; legal review of the contract by either or both buyer's and seller's lawyers; home appraises for purchase amount or less; your ability to obtain a specified mortgage loan within a specified time at an agreed-upon interest rate and points (financing contingency).

You, as a potential buyer, start the process by putting an offer with price and terms in writing and presenting it to the seller through your buyer's agent. Buying a home is probably the biggest financial investment you will make. Only you can decide which home you want, and the price is up to you and the seller.

◆ ◆ ◆

Essential Takeaway

Essential Takeaway: Before you put in an offer to purchase a home, understand that the seller has three basic options: (1) accept your offer, (2) counteroffer on specific details or (3) reject your offer. If there is any negotiation, it usually takes place trading counteroffers if the seller doesn't immediately accept or reject the offer. Keep up the dialogue until you arrive at the price you can pay and the price and terms the seller can accept. This is where a buyer's agent's help is invaluable. Your agent keeps the negotiation process running smoothly. With knowledge of both your situation and the seller's, plus a complete understanding of financing options, an agent can suggest strategies that bring about a satisfactory transaction and a signed contract!

◆ ◆ ◆

Sweat The Small Stuff To Get Agreement

First, prove you mean business. There are few better ways to show a seller you are serious about buying a property than by including a good-faith deposit along with your offer. A competitive deposit could be a few thousand dollars to as much as 5% of your bid price to be sure it gets the seller's attention. Your agent will guide you.

Keep it simple and clean. Make sure your headache-free contract itself isn't messy or overly cluttered with unnecessary contingencies, especially specific repairs. Keep contingencies to a minimum. Better yet, offer to be helpful, such as by ordering an inspection within 48 hours or being willing to take care of any required local certificates such as smoke detectors or water safety. Be flexible. A buyer who will accommodate a seller's needs is a smart buyer.

CONTINGENCIES PROTECT YOUR POSITION IN A HOME PURCHASE

Buyers are still in the driver's seat in many real estate markets around the country. That puts them at an advantage when it comes to negotiating the terms of their home-purchase contracts.

Your buyer's agent can ensure that your offer and the final contract include the types of contingencies[††] that will protect your interests and even allow you to back away from a deal that isn't meeting your expectations. Following are the three most common contract contingencies buyers opt to include.

> [††] *Contingency*
> A requirement of the purchase contract that nullifies the contract if the contingency is not met.

Inspection. A home-inspection contingency can save you a lot of money in the long run, yet it may be the first contingency you're tempted to drop if you find yourself competing against other buyers for a home. It's wise to hang onto this contingency — even if you have to offer more money in the contract to do so.

Remember that although sellers may have to disclose known defects in their home, they often aren't aware of everything that's wrong with it. Why risk thousands of dollars in repair costs that could have been avoided with a pre-settlement inspection?

Financing. A financing contingency simply states that the contract is void if you, the buyer, cannot obtain a specified type of mortgage at a certain rate (or better) within a specified period of time. Few sellers balk at this contract provision if the terms stated are reasonable, and especially if you are already pre-approved for a mortgage. Failing to include this contingency could cost you plenty if rates unexpectedly shoot up or your personal financial situation changes suddenly before settlement.

Appraisal. Another contingency you should consider covers appraisals. If your lender's appraisal comes in lower than the price you've agreed to with the seller, you would have the opportunity (depending on how the contingency is written) to get out of the contract, increase your down payment, split the difference with the seller, or renegotiate the sales price. In today's market, with unstable home values, an appraisal contingency can be essential.

How To Behave Yourself Once You Submit An Offer

With the help of your buyer's agent, you've crafted a great offer and turned it over to the sellers and their agent. Let the knuckle-biting begin — but stay focused.

● Rely on your agent to keep negotiations moving forward. Your trusted real estate pro knows what you want — and what you are willing to give sellers — and is in a unique position to help negotiations along.

● Respond quickly to a counteroffer once you've had a chance to review it thoroughly. When sellers make a counteroffer, they are anxiously awaiting your response, but moods can change quickly. You may want to accept the offer if it meets your needs, or you may want to respond with another counteroffer. Even if you consider the first counteroffer unacceptable, keep the dialogue going; after all, their initial counteroffer demonstrates that they are willing to work with you. It's not unusual to exchange two or three counteroffers before a contract is reached.

● Exercise confidence and patience as the seller weighs your counteroffers. Be forthcoming with all information requested and call attention to all the areas of agreement. Stay positive. When disagreements occur, iron out all the small negotiation areas before getting down to any real stumbling block later on, after most items are agreed upon.

Avoid This Costly Negotiating Mistake: **Turning the process into an extreme kick-boxing match to the death.**

Solution: Keep in mind that you, the seller, and your agents all want the same thing — a successful home-sale transaction. Here are three win-win-win tips:

1. Only negotiate the facts.

2. Identify potential problems in the contract, but don't negotiate the repairs until estimates have been made. (Consider eliminating the repair requests if they're minor, or lumping them all into one repair budget amount.)

3. Stick to the essential issues — avoid negotiating little details at the outset that you don't care much about. You may have an opportunity to add them in with later counteroffers.

MULTIPLE PURCHASE OFFERS COULD WORK TO YOUR ADVANTAGE

During the housing boom, where demand was sky high compared to the low inventory of homes for sale, it wasn't uncommon for a home seller to receive multiple offers from different buyers. Then, sellers were in the happy position of being able to pick the best offer that came in.

Today, the tables have turned in some markets. Your time has come, cowboy. Here is how some buyers root out the best value by making multiple, simultaneous purchase offers on several different homes. In this multiple-offer scenario, sellers compete for the buyer's contract. The buyer gets to pick the best of the counteroffers that come back approved by the sellers.

For a buyer to make several simultaneous offers on different homes, the offers must always include a special clause declaring the offer not valid until the buyer approves — again, within a specified time frame. In this case, the offer is validated by the seller and returned to the buyer, but the contract only becomes ratified when the buyer approves it. Normally, a buyer's purchase offer is valid during the offer period — the time stipulated for the seller to respond in, say, 48 hours. If the seller signs the offer, a contract is created.

Multiple purchase offers are not for everyone. Talk with your buyer's agent to find out whether a multiple-offer strategy could work for you in your market.

Competition Can Heat Things Up Don't lose your head. Just because the market is active doesn't mean you should be willing to pay any amount to get your dream home.

Sometimes in the heat of the battle — think bidding war — the competition from other buyers can change your perception and make you lose focus on your goals.

Don't try to "win" the home if it means paying more than you had planned to. Refer back to your maximum price amount and your pre-approved loan amount (which may actually be more than you want to spend).

Sure, you may have to offer something other than the asking price, such as paying some or all points, inspections or closing costs, or offering a settlement date that fits the seller's timetable. But don't go crazy. Remember: You may have to sell this home one day, and overpaying now will make it harder to get your value back when you sell.

> **Four Smart Ways To Avoid Losing A Bidding War**

You are not alone if you're looking for a rock-bottom price on a home in today's market. Be careful, though, in your pursuit of that attractive property that's priced so low it attracts gobs of attention. You could end up in a competitive bidding situation that leaves you with a contract price above the property's true market value. And that could spell trouble when your appraisal comes back below the price you agreed to with the seller. How do you protect yourself?

1. **Be sure a buyer's agent represents you.** This bears repeating, as we mentioned in Chapter 1 BUY SMART: It's essential to have a top-notch buyer's agent on your side. A licensed buyer's agent will be bound to provide you with all the information at their disposal about the properties you're considering and to represent your interests — not the seller's (or the new home builder's) — in negotiations to purchase.

2. **Ask your buyer's agent for an analysis of the property's value.** Your agent will look at the recent sales prices of comparable homes as well as those of homes that failed to sell (expireds are a key market indicator of what price is too high). The agent will also know what else is currently on the market, how those listing prices compare with the property you want and local price trends.

3. **Set a maximum price you're willing to pay.** It's easy to get caught up in a bidding war once you've decided a home is absolutely the one for you. If you've set a realistic ceiling, remind yourself that you did so for some very good reasons, and don't go beyond that price just to walk away with the winning contract.

4. **Remember, there are plenty of alternatives available.** You may not have seen that next perfect home yet, but with patience and discipline you will eventually find the one that meets all your requirements — and at a great price, too. *Smart Tip:* In a hot market nobody wants their offer languishing in an e-mail inbox or on a fax machine in the listing agent's office while other buyers are putting offers on the seller's kitchen table. When the situation calls for that personal touch, you'll gain an advantage by having your buyer's agent

present your offer in person. Additionally, your real estate pro may pick up critical intelligence on any competing offers or a possible bidding war by being on the scene.

HOW TO USE COUNTEROFFERS TO SECURE YOUR PERFECT HOME

Smart buyers only offer terms in their counteroffers that will help move or close the contract. Your goal is to purchase the home for the best price.

Perhaps a seller is unwilling to negotiate on price because the home is already priced fairly. Instead of asking for a price reduction, you can counteroffer with a concession,[††] or deal sweetener.

> [††] *Concession*
> A benefit that can favor a buyer or seller in a real estate transaction. Items negotiated may have a cost or be material items. Some sellers may put these "sweeteners" in the original listing to attract buyer interest. Other sweeteners can be held up the seller's sleeve until a purchase offer comes in; then the seller can add them into counteroffers. *Smart Tip:* As a smart buyer, you can ask outright for some of these sweeteners in addition to or in place of price concessions in your purchase offer.

Of course, not all properties, nor all sellers or neighborhoods, require sweeteners. Your buyer's agent can advise you whether or not to use any of the following contract terms for your specific situation.

Settlement Sweeteners

Points. Sellers may pay some or all of the buyer's points, which benefits you, the home buyer, in three ways. First, when the seller pays some points, the amount of cash you need at settlement is reduced. Second, you get a sizable tax write-off, as many buyers now can deduct as a "Schedule A mortgage expense" the points sellers pay for them at closing. Third, the interest rate for the loan may be lower. When the seller pays points for you, you are better able to finance the agreed-upon sale price.

● **Closing costs.** Sellers can offer, instead, to pay part of the closing/settlement costs (for title search, attorney's services, appraisal, recording fees, etc.) that you would ordinarily pay.

● **Furnishings.** Some sellers, if asked, may include with the purchase price such items as household furnishings, a swing set, sandbox, tractor-mower or draperies tailored to specific windows. These may be included in a separate contract addendum.

● **Home warranty.** Ask for a home warranty to help you feel protected. For as little as $300, the seller can provide a one-year warranty that covers all the home's major systems. Some programs even cover appliances. That said, be sure to negotiate a low or no deductible to minimize your costs should you have to make a claim.

| **Accommodations** | Accommodations are small favors the seller can grant you to help you overcome logistical obstacles. |

● **Occupancy.** Work out pre-occupancy or post-occupancy terms if date of occupancy is a problem for you or the seller.

● **Move in.** Some sellers will consider occupying temporary living quarters themselves in order to let the buyer move in on schedule.

● **Storage.** Some sellers may be open to assisting in a reasonable way with your problems in transferring household items (for example, storing items in the garage, accepting delivery of appliances, etc.).

● **Services.** Ask about the availability of continuing services for lawn care, home security systems or house cleaning that may have been paid ahead.

| **Loan Sweeteners** | ● **Buy-down.** Some sellers will consider buying down the initial interest rate for serious purchasers so they can qualify for a loan. |

● **Assumption.** Ask if the seller has an assumable loan with a below-market interest rate that they might consider making available to you. Be sure to check the lender's loan assumption requirements.

● **Take-back.** Some sellers might even be in a position to offer you a second mortgage by taking back some of the purchase price in a note. It doesn't hurt to ask.

● **Seller financing.** Other sellers might be able to hold the first mortgage for you. They may be inclined to do this if they own the home free and clear and if mortgage rates are higher than the current return on other investment options.

● **Lease/purchase.** Another option, if you can't qualify for a loan or there are other problems with getting to settlement, is to rent the home with a delayed settlement, provided you are sure you will eventually qualify for the loan. Negotiate with the seller to have part of the rent amount apply to the down payment.

Some of these strategies may seem excessive to you. However, many smart buyers have seen them pay off, putting cash in their pocket. *Smart Tip:* When you're shopping for a home, the best advice that bears repeating is to get pre-approved for a mortgage. That way you know exactly how much you can afford to finance—and also what your acceptable concession limit is (according to your lender) so you know exactly how much you may accept from the seller before negotiations begin.

Costly Concessions Mistake To Avoid

Mistake: Negotiating too much in the way of seller contributions/concessions. Rather than lowering the home's price to get it sold, you and the seller negotiate for the seller to pay for some closing costs, loan points, a redecorating allowance, etc. Everyone is happy—except your lender, who says you can only take up to, say, 3% of the home's sale price in seller contributions. Now your loan is in jeopardy! If the seller's contribution/concession is deemed non-allowable by your lender, the loan underwriters may reduce the value of the home by the amount of the contribution (or some portion of it) and reduce your loan size accordingly—effectively nullifying the advantage of the contribution for you.

Solution: Seller contributions are very tempting to buyers, as they usually reduce the buyer's cash outlay. While these offers may be appealing as you shop for a home—particularly if you're strapped for cash—avoid the temptation to accept too much. Find out ahead of time exactly how much in seller contributions your lender will allow.

Cue the soaring chorus of angels! The seller ratified your offer! Time to celebrate! Not so fast. Before you blast the news to all your friends, take a deep breath. You'll need a survivor's guide to minimize costs and hiccups getting from contract to closing/settlement. On to the homestretch in Chapter 7!

Chapter 6 Roundup

Smart Essentials NEGOTIATE :: What You Have Learned

▶▶ How to craft an irresistible purchase offer.
▶▶ Sweat the small stuff to get agreement.
▶▶ Know how contingencies protect your position in a home purchase.
▶▶ Avoid costly negotiating mistakes.
▶▶ Multiple purchase offers can work to your advantage as a buyer.
▶▶ How to beat the competition when a bidding war heats up.
▶▶ Use counteroffers to reel in your perfect contract.

CHAPTER 7

CLOSE

In this chapter, you will learn smarts ways to:

1. Save on brokerage fees, title insurance, points and junk fees.

2. Know what to expect with your home inspection.

3. Avoid costly closing mistakes that can kill your deal.

SURVIVAL GUIDE TO MINIMIZE COSTS FROM CONTRACT TO CLOSING

We talked a lot about closing costs in Chapter 4 MONEY. At closing/settlement is where the money hits the fan. While you're biting your nails over whether the deal will hang together, now is the time to beat the buzzer on loan fees, pre-paids, escrows, title expenses, recording costs, settlement fees and sometimes items paid outside of closing (POC). Yikes! Just how to minimize your costs — and avoid costly gotchas from contract to closing — is the subject of this essential last chapter. Home stretch, baby! Hang on!

Small Tips To Save Big At Closing Time

As you dance through the minefield toward closing/settlement, you want to ensure there are no surprises, especially financial ones. Rely on your buyer's agent and loan officer — and keep these tips in mind.

● **Loan amount gotcha.** When all is signed and dated, one of the smartest strategies to keep from paying cash at the closing table (and keep more money in your pocket) is to add your closing costs into the loan amount you borrow. This is called "financing" your costs. The rub comes in the timing. At the time of your application you need to anticipate the amount of closing costs (or come pretty close using the GFE) and arrange with your lender to increase the loan amount to cover those costs. (You'll pay any minimal extra with a check.) Don't expect to change your loan amount at the settlement table. *Smart Tip:* By not applying for the max you are approved to borrow you will leave some room to add in your closing costs to your loan amount.

● **Private mortgage insurance gotcha.** If you don't make at least a 20% down payment, the lender will require you to buy private mortgage insurance (PMI). You can pay monthly or for the entire year in a lump sum up front (government-backed loans may require both) — forever until your equity grows to 20%, which takes a long time. Generally, PMI rates vary between 0.5% to 1% of the loan amount per year ($100,000 loan x 1% = $1,000 PMI every year). PMI rates vary by your amount of down payment (higher down payment, lower PMI), loan type (fixed, adjustable, etc.) and if the loan is sub-prime or jumbo. Whatever the cost, PMI is a gotcha you can avoid. *Smart Tip:* You can avoid PMI when you: (1) Assemble cash to make a 20% down payment. (2) Get a second mortgage to use for part of the down payment. For example, you can get an 80/10/10 loan (80% loan, 10% second mortgage and 10% down) or a variation thereof and sidestep PMI. (3) Finance the PMI by adding the one-time upfront fee to the outstanding loan balance. Some lenders will discount your PMI for paying up front. (4) Ask if your lender will waive PMI if you pay a higher interest rate, say, 0.75% to 1% more, depending on the down payment. The advantage is mortgage interest is tax-deductible, but PMI is not unless you itemize and earn less than $110,000. (BTW, don't confuse Private Mortgage Insurance, which insures the lender against loss if you default, with Mortgage Life Insurance, which pays off the loan if you die.)

● **Buyer's agent fee gotcha.** Real estate brokerage fees are negotiable and rates are competitive. Some discount brokers knock a percent or two off the average commission rate and provide fewer services. Some individual agents may lower their commission to get a coveted listing. Those discounts could cost you — the home buyer — money if you buy a home with buyer's agent.

Why? Traditionally, the commission paid by a seller was split between the "listing" broker (and his or her agent who marketed the home for the seller) and the "selling" broker (and the agent who worked with the buyer). In reality, both sets of brokers/agents worked for the seller. (All states today require agents to disclose which party they represent in various scenarios.) Now when you hire a buyer's agent, that agent is truly working for you. Many full-service brokers do split half the listing commission paid by the seller with buyer's agents — encouraging them to bring buyers to the home. But when the seller-paid commission has been discounted, the buyer's agent may end up with a lot less than the fee stipulated in the contract with you. And you — the buyer — could end up paying the difference. *Smart Tip:* Be sure to discuss this buyer-paid scenario with your buyer's agent before signing the agency agreement. If you absolutely only want the buyer's agent services at no cost, then one option is to forego buying any home where the seller or a discounted commission doesn't pay your buyer's agent's full fee. Also discuss how to resolve this gotcha, perhaps by negotiating further with the seller or financing the fee.

● **Title insurance gotcha.** A lien is a constraint placed on the title of a property that allows the lienholder to recover money the owner owes out of the home-sale proceeds. For example, your first mortgage is a lien that allows the lender to force the sale of your home if you default on your mortgage (foreclosure). A home-equity-backed loan would constitute a second lien on your home, which would be paid after the first lien holder's claim has been satisfied. In fact, a property can have any number of liens placed on it. Others, such as the Internal Revenue Service, creditors, contractors, homeowners associations and local taxing authorities, can also seek judgments to get property liens.

A title search may reveal encumbrances on the property title like tax liens, easements, leases or an undisclosed co-owner. Avoid this trap by having the title search done early to confirm clear title, if possible. But mistakes can happen. That's why your lender will require that you purchase lender's title insurance to cover the lender's interest in your home. *Smart Tip:* Be sure to beat the gotcha of title problems by buying an owner's title policy to cover your own interests — a one-time cost that provides protection as long as you own the property. If you already own a home, consider contacting the title insurance company you used before and ask what their rate is for repeat business. The recent spate of foreclosures and short sales makes this precaution all-important. *Bonus Smart Tip:* Be sure to read exceptions under the "Schedule B" of your owner's title policy. Some policies will not cover disputes about ownership that result from a foreclosure proceeding. Purchasing an "enhanced title policy" may be your best bet, as it will cover more of the risks you could face down the road.

● **Homeowners insurance gotcha.** Lenders require you to carry a homeowners insurance policy (also "hazard insurance") to protect your home (and the lender's money) against such hazards as fire, smoke, wind, hail, explosion, riot, theft, glass breakage (if the glass is part of the home) and damage caused by aircraft, vehicles or vandalism. A basic policy also protects you against injury to a visitor on your property. An "all-risk" policy reimburses you for the major hazards plus damage due to lesser catastrophes such as burst water pipes. But, to insure all your equity and personal property, you may still need additional coverage. *Smart Tip:* A "guaranteed replacement cost" policy covers your home and contents for the full replacement value, rather than the actual cash value (the replacement cost minus depreciation). Consider a policy with an "inflation guard" to adjust the amount of coverage based on the inflation rate.

● **Discount points gotcha.** A loan discount point is equal to 1% of the loan amount. Thus, on a $100,000 loan, a borrower would pay $1,000 per point to the lender. Discount points are charged to increase a lender's yield and you get a lower interest rate—a discounted rate. Paying one point may get you a 1/8% to 1/4% drop in interest rate, depending on the current market. The lower rate reduces your monthly payment and long-term interest expense of the loan.

Lingo gotcha: Some lenders quote service fees such as an origination or application fee in terms of "points"—each point equals 1% of the loan amount; such fees are not tax-deductible. Don't confuse service "points" with discount points, which are deductible as prepaid interest.

Many borrowers opt not to pay points if they are short of cash or they don't expect to own the home for long. *Smart Tip:* Negotiate with your seller to pay the discount points, in effect "buying down" the rate. How? Agree to the seller's price, if the seller will pay your discount points. Seller gets full price; you get a lower payment. It gets better: Seller-paid points are tax-deductible for the buyer. Consult your tax adviser or IRS Publication 936 "Home Mortgage Interest Deduction," for further details. *Smart Bonus Tip:* If the seller won't bite or you are short of cash, roll the points into your mortgage loan. The higher tax deduction on your interest payments will further increase the savings achieved by buying down the rate. Sweet.

● **Hidden junk-fees gotcha.** Some lenders add questionable charges at closing that were not shown on the Truth-In-Lending form, such as an underwriting fee, loan disbursement charges, tax service fee, courier fees or mark-ups on court documentation fees. *Smart Tip:* Avoid these fees by asking the lender at application time exactly what fees are included on the federal settlement forms and what additional fees may be charged at settlement or closing. Some of these fees can be negotiated down or waived for the customer who complains. But it's best to drive your bargain before you make your loan application.

● **Home-inspection gotcha.** Don't assume that a thoroughly completed disclosure statement includes everything you need to know about the property. Sellers and their agents can only divulge information they are aware of or suspect may be true. *Smart Tip:* Professional home inspectors may find defects that homeowners had no inkling about. The best advice for buyers — even more important when properties are being sold "as is" — is to have the property inspected by a licensed professional. Use the written report and repair estimates to negotiate a repair clause in your contract. If there are numerous small repairs, lump them into one figure and accept a check or cash concession at settlement/closing. *Bonus Smart Tip:* You may want to hire special topic-specific expert inspector(s) to check your home for termites/pests, mold, radon, asbestos, etc., depending on the age, location and condition of the home. These inspectors are specially trained to thoroughly inspect a home for conditions that general inspectors are not trained for.

◆ ◆ ◆

Essential Takeaway: *Buying without a home inspection isn't a smart move. Some buyers don't add a home-inspection contingency, so their contract looks better than their competitors'. While this might sound like a good strategy in a hot market, it can come back to bite the buyer — or even the seller. Some sellers have wound up in court after accepting a contract without a home inspection because after-sale inspections of their homes revealed serious defects, prompting the buyers to take legal action for relief.*

Essential Takeaway

◆ ◆ ◆

● **Survey gotcha.** The property survey may show that the lot boundaries are different from the property plat, a neighbor's fence is over the line or zoning regulations have been violated. Avoid the gotcha by asking to see the seller's survey made back when the seller bought the house, and go over any additions or variations with your real estate agent. Also, have your new survey done early. *Smart Tip:* A property survey is a common safeguard required by mortgage lenders to ensure there are no property-line problems. In cash transactions, however, buyers may be tempted to skip this precaution. A survey can show defects, such as a neighbor's shed placed over the line or violations of zoning regulations. If these are discovered, the seller should be responsible for correcting them.

● **Walk-through gotcha.** Once all contract contingencies are fulfilled and the paperwork is ready for signing, the final step is for the buyer to conduct a walk-through of the property. At this point, the buyer makes sure the property is in the condition it is supposed to be in according to the sales contract. Remember, a walk-through is not a second inspection. Most homes show some wear and tear — especially after the sellers have just moved out. Be aware that an early walk-through can cause problems, especially if the sellers haven't removed all their personal property. An area rug, for instance, may be hiding a defect in the flooring, or furniture may conceal damaged walls. Or the sellers could leave behind lots of junk they didn't want — another headache for you.

Smart Tip: Time a walk-through after the sellers have moved out, but before closing/settlement. Have your buyer's agent accompany you, or pay your inspector to join you to ensure any required repairs have been made properly. Take along the list of agreed-upon items that convey or need repair to check them off. Any problems that arise must be negotiated at the settlement/closing table. But be prepared to set a dollar amount for an escrow fund for items that fall through the cracks.

● **Credit score gotcha.** As you're getting down to the wire and ready to close on your home, ensure you do everything to keep your mortgage application from being delayed or rejected. Remember: All credit inquiries are not alike.

"Soft pull" inquiries are those not associated with an effort to secure new credit. For example, a company checking your credit report to determine whether to send you a credit card would be a soft pull. So would an instance of you checking your own credit report for accuracy, or a potential employer checking your report as part of a background check. These soft pulls have no effect on your credit score.

"Hard pull" inquiries, on the other hand, are report requests that you've approved to obtain new credit, such as taking out a car loan, opening a new credit card account, applying for a mortgage, etc. Excessive hard pulls over a several-month period could affect your credit score significantly, as they may indicate you've had multiple credit rejections or taken on credit obligations that have yet to appear in your credit report.

Smart Tip: Avoid applying for credit accounts before your mortgage is closed/settled. FICO recommends that consumers shopping for a particular type of credit should concentrate their efforts so all credit inquiries show up in a fairly compressed time frame—not longer than 45 days—and can be related to a single reason, such as a home purchase or refinancing.

HOW TO AVOID SABOTAGING YOUR MORTGAGE CLOSING

We've seen buyers innocently, yet adversely, hurt their credit score right when they are waiting to close their mortgage and home. Remember, back in Chapter 4 MONEY, how you learned smart ways to avoid lender rejection like minimizing debt and avoiding last-minute gaffes? Here are some of those don't-do gaffes you want to avoid at all cost from the moment of mortgage application through signing at closing/settlement.

1. Don't order any furniture or appliances for a new home even if no payment is immediately due, such as the no-payment-until-next-year deals.

2. Don't let any stores run a credit check for a new credit card when you're shopping or looking for new furniture or appliances.

3. Don't apply for new credit cards, even when stores offer a discount for doing so.

4. Pay all credit card bills on time, even if it means paying utility bills late.

5. Refuse increases in your credit limit if the increase is more than you need or is high in relation to your income.

6. Pay off and close any existing accounts with finance companies, since they're viewed negatively in the scoring (Tips 6 and 7 are ideally completed before you submit your loan application).

7. Maintain at least one of your oldest cards to show a lengthy credit history.

WHAT TO EXPECT AT SETTLEMENT OR CLOSING

In some areas, you and your buyer's agent meet with the sellers, their agent, a settlement or closing officer and sometimes attorneys representing the seller and/or you, to settle the transfer of the property and close the transaction. In other areas, an escrow officer does all the preparations for closing, and contacts the buyer and seller to come in individually and sign their respective documents.

In either case, you will need to provide:

- ▶ Your homeowners insurance policy and paid receipt for one year's coverage, sometimes paid at settlement or closing.
- ▶ A certified or cashier's check for the balance of your down payment and your settlement or closing costs. Find out who the check should be made payable to.
- ▶ Your regular check book so that you can pay any incidental costs. Typically all settlement or closing costs are calculated in advance and your certified check is usually sufficient.

You go over a list of adjustments presented on government-standard "Settlement Statements" to settle what you and the seller owe each other in cash, taxes, etc. You sign the mortgage and a mortgage note (denoting your monthly principal and interest payments). Don't ignore the fine print. Purchasing a home is the largest investment most of us ever make. That's why understanding what you're signing is imperative! If you don't understand something about the sales contract, don't hesitate to ask for an explanation from your buyer's agent or closing officer. The same advice applies to your mortgage loan.

Smart Tip: Insist on seeing the settlement sheets the day before settlement or closing. That way, you'll avoid last-minute problems — such as an interest rate or points other than you agreed to showing up on the paperwork. Sometimes missing the settlement date because of an eleventh-hour snag endangers the locked-in interest rate or the entire sale. Don't get trapped by a too-close settlement or closing. Get a 60-day lock-in for your loan interest rate, if possible, and give yourself that much time to close/settle the sale.

After all documents are signed by both parties and you pay the seller, the transaction will be recorded at the local courthouse, and you'll receive the keys. Be sure you also get all the little things, including mailbox key, garage door opener(s) and code, gate key/code, codes for alarms/security systems, etc. The home is yours!

Yee haw! You did it! You bought your home at the best price and the lowest payment. Relax. You've earned it. Enjoy your new nest . . . and let us hear what advice you would share with other Smarties setting out on the same adventure.

CONGRATULATIONS!

Chapter 7 Roundup

Smart Essentials CLOSE :: What You Have Learned

►► Title insurance: playing it safe.
►► What kind of homeowners insurance should I carry?
►► Smart ways to know when to buy down your interest rate.
►► How to spot and avoid hidden junk fees.
►► Finding a reliable home inspector.
►► Walk-through tips to identify problems before buying.
►► How to avoid costly survey surprises.
►► Credit score-sabatoging moves not to make.
►► What to expect at the settlement table.

Smart Essentials

Page   **Essential Note**

About The Series

SMART ESSENTIALS was written for you.

We know because you tell us. Our readers are smart, busy, capable people stressed by the fact that they only get one chance to get it right buying or selling real estate. You tell us on our *http://www.SmartEssentials.com* website and in your emails. You appreciate smart, useful, distilled information that goes straight to the point.

Certainly, our readers *can* swim through the tides of endless online articles searching for useful information. Certainly, our readers *can* slog through full-length how-to books trying to glean the chapter here or there — hidden in the general filler — that they really need. But you're too smart for that. You appreciate concise ideas that can make you tens of thousands in profit when you sell real estate and save you thousands at the settlement table when you buy — or that help you avoid costly mistakes you didn't have to make.

You want the information now. You want it smartly presented. You want it current for today's market. Mostly you want your information concise, concentrated and applicable to your situation.

● Like the frenzied bride who thanked us for advising that engaged couples should start looking for a home three months *after* the wedding.

● Like the Canadian investor who appreciated learning that California charges a transfer tax on non-resident sales, so he bought in Nevada.

● Like the thankful divorced Dad who bought two extra bedrooms for sleepovers on custody weekends.

● And like the thankful parents who saved thousands over seven years (supporting two college kids) by investing in rentable student housing because at their state university, most students had to rent off-campus housing.

We also know most of our readers typically buy multiple SMART ESSENTIALS, not only because most sellers are buyers and most buyers become sellers, but mostly because you have smart friends. You talk. Naturally. After all, you just spent the last few months consumed by one of the largest life-shaping transactions of your life. Who wouldn't need to vent?

That's why we wrote every SMART ESSENTIALS for you.

Let us know what you think. More important, when you run across one of those incredible little nuggets of street-smart wisdom during your transaction, email us or share it as a Smarties' Story on our website. We love your stories. And the thousands of other Smarties facing the same situation will thank you, too. Giving is sharing. And sharing is the best way we know to enhance love.

Looking forward to hearing from you!

Dan Gooder Richard
Series Editor

Dan Gooder Richard can be contacted at:

SMART ESSENTIALS
c/o Inkspiration Media
2724 Dorr Avenue, Suite 103
Fairfax, VA 22031
(703) 698-7750
BuyingAHome@SmartEssentials.com
http://www.SmartEssentials.com

About The Team

A venture the size of SMART ESSENTIALS requires an outstanding team. Dan Gooder Richard is the editor of the SMART ESSENTIALS series. Dan's first book, REAL ESTATE RAINMAKER®: Successful Strategies for Real Estate Marketing, was published by John Wiley & Sons in 2000. Dan's second book, REAL ESTATE RAINMAKER®: Guide to Online Marketing, was published by John Wiley & Sons in 2004. He is also creator of the RAINMAKER LEAD SYSTEM® now in use by thousands of real estate professionals nationwide. He and his wife, Synnove Granholm, founded GOODER GROUP® in 1983 and continue to manage the Fairfax, Virginia-based publisher of marketing materials for real estate and mortgage professionals. Amy J. Hausman, our marketing diva and author of this BUYING guide, keeps the buzz going with every new publication. Hats off to Deborah Rhoney, our managing editor and principal writer. She puts the smart into the essentials. Special thanks to our Web master, Tammy Waitsman, and our social media guru, Jesse Hickman, for making the online side of SMART ESSENTIALS truly click. Jane Rooney, our controller at Inkspiration Media, keeps us on track and on forecast. Stephanie Simmons keeps the service to readers stellar and makes the smallest detail her mission. A special thanks to David Wu, of DW Design, whose branding and graphic design make us all look good. To the entire team at SMART ESSENTIALS — thank you — we couldn't do it without you!

SMARTIE'S CREED

🗩 **I will express my voice** at *http://www.SmartEssentials.com* and become part of the world's smartest communities.

🗩 **I will help others get smarter for less.** I simply share with two. And they tell two. If we pay it forward 33 times, we can reach every person in the world.

🗩 **I will keep up to date** and with one click, one post, one random act of selflessness, I will be smarter, happier, richer.

🗩 **I can imagine** where everyone reading my voice did something today to improve others. The world would be a smarter place . . . and it all would be thanks to my original, selfless act to help others.

SMART TALK

We know we're biased. But we think our Smartie community members are smart, outspoken and generous. You can learn a lot about home buying from them, and they from you. Come share your insights and experiences and questions at http://www.SmartEssentials.com. *We'll all be smarter for it!*

Pay it forward at *http://www.SmartEssentials.com* today!

More Titles In The Best-Selling SMART ESSENTIALS Series

🗩 SMART ESSENTIALS FOR SELLING YOUR HOME
How To Get The Highest Price In The Shortest Time

🗩 SMART ESSENTIALS FOR BUYING A HOME
How To Get The Best Price And The Lowest Payment

🗩 SMART ESSENTIALS FOR REAL ESTATE INVESTING
How To Build Wealth In Rental Property Today

🗩 SMART ESSENTIALS FOR BUYING FORECLOSURES
Finding Hidden Bargains For Home Or Profit

🗩 SMART ESSENTIALS FOR COLLEGE RENTALS
Parent and Investor Guide To Buying College-Town Real Estate

www.ingramcontent.com/pod-product-compliance
Lightning Source LLC
Chambersburg PA
CBHW071440210326
41597CB00020B/3881